BEYOND THE VEIL

Unveiling Christ's Fullness

A Study of Hebrews

Jack W. Hayford
with
Joseph Snider

THOMAS NELSON PUBLISHERS
Nashville • Atlanta • London • Vancouver

DEDICATION

This, the third series of *Spirit-Filled Life
Bible Study Guides*, is dedicated to the
memory of

Dr. Roy H. Hicks, Jr.
(1944–1994)

one of God's "men for all seasons,"
faithful in the Word, mighty in the Spirit,
leading multitudes into the love of God
and the worship of His Son, Jesus Christ.

Unto Christ's glory and in Roy's memory,
we will continue to sing:

> *Praise the Name of Jesus,*
> *Praise the Name of Jesus,*
> *He's my Rock, He's my Fortress,*
> *He's my Deliverer, in Him will I trust.*
> *Praise the Name of Jesus.*

Words by Roy Hicks, Jr., © 1976 by Latter Rain Music.
All rights administered by The Sparrow Corporation. All rights reserved. Used by permission.

**Beyond the Veil: Unveiling Christ's Fullness
A Study of Hebrews**
Copyright © 1994 by Jack W. Hayford

Published in Nashville, Tennessee, by Thomas Nelson, Inc.

Unless otherwise indicated, Scripture quotations are from the
New King James Version of the Bible, © 1979, 1980, 1982,
Thomas Nelson, Inc., Publishers

Printed in the United States of America
1 2 3 4 5 6 7 8 — 00 99 98 97 96 95 94

CONTENTS

About the Executive Editor/About the Writer 4

The Gift That Keeps on Giving 5

Lesson 1: The Best Revelation (1:1—2:4) 10

Lesson 2: The Best Man (2:5–18) 21

Lesson 3: The Best Hope for Peace with God (3:1—4:13) ... 31

Lesson 4: The Best Help During Temptation (4:14—5:11) 44

Lesson 5: The Best Cure for Immaturity (5:12—6:20) 57

Lesson 6: The Best Access to God (7:1–28) 71

Lesson 7: The Best Promise Made by God (8:1–13) 82

Lesson 8: The Best Purification (9:1–28) 91

Lesson 9: The Best Sacrifice for Sin (10:1–18) 104

Lesson 10: The Best Assurance of Salvation (10:19–39) 115

Lesson 11: The Best Object of Faith (11:1–40) 125

Lesson 12: The Best Way to Follow Jesus (12:1–29) 137

Lesson 13: The Best Shepherd (13:1–25) 149

Beyond the Veil: Unveiling Christ's Fullness (A Study of Hebrews) is one of a series of study guides that focus exciting, discovery-geared coverage of Bible book and power themes—all prompting toward dynamic, Holy Spirit-filled living.

About the Executive Editor

JACK W. HAYFORD, noted pastor, teacher, writer, and composer, is the Executive Editor of the complete series, working with the publisher in the conceiving and developing of each of the books.

Dr. Hayford is Senior Pastor of The Church On The Way, the First Foursquare Church of Van Nuys, California. He and his wife, Anna, have four married children, all of whom are active in either pastoral ministry or vital church life. As General Editor of the *Spirit-Filled Life Bible*, Pastor Hayford led a four-year project, which has resulted in the availability of one of today's most practical and popular study Bibles. He is author of more than twenty books, including *A Passion for Fullness, The Beauty of Spiritual Language, Rebuilding the Real You,* and *Prayer Is Invading the Impossible.* His musical compositions number over four hundred songs, including the widely sung "Majesty."

About the Writer

JOSEPH SNIDER has worked in Christian ministry for more than twenty years. In addition to freelance writing and speaking, he worked three years with Young Life, served for seven years on the Christian Education faculty at Fort Wayne Bible College, and pastored churches in Indianapolis and Fort Wayne, Indiana. He currently enjoys part-time teaching at Franklin College in Franklin, Indiana. His writing includes material for Thomas Nelson Publishers, Moody Magazine, Union Gospel Press, and David C. Cook.

Married to Sally Snider, Joe has two grown children, Jenny and Ted. They live in Indianapolis, Indiana. Joe earned a B.A. in English from Cedarville College in Cedarville, Ohio, and a Th.M. in Christian Education from Dallas Theological Seminary.

Of this contributor, the General Editor has remarked: "Joe Snider's strength and stability as a gracious, godly man comes through in his writing. His perceptive and practical way of pointing the way to truth inspires students of God's Word."

THE GIFT
THAT KEEPS ON GIVING

Who doesn't like presents? Whether they come wrapped in colorful paper and beautiful bows, or brown paper bags closed and tied at the top with old shoestring. Kids and adults of all ages love getting and opening presents.

But even this moment of surprise and pleasure can be marked by dread and fear. All it takes is for these words to appear: "Assembly Required. Instructions Enclosed." How we hate these words! They taunt us, tease us, beckon us to try to challenge them, all the while knowing that they have the upper hand. If we don't understand the instructions, or if we ignore them and try to put the gift together ourselves, more than likely we'll only assemble frustration and anger. What we felt about our great gift—all the joy, anticipation, and wonder—will vanish. And they will never return, at least not to that pristine state they had before we realized that *we* had to assemble our present with instructions *no consumer* will ever understand.

One of the most precious gifts God has given us is His Word, the Bible. Wrapped in the glory and sacrifice of His Son and delivered by the power and ministry of His Spirit, it is a treasured gift—one the family of God has preserved and protected for centuries as a family heirloom. It promises that it is the gift that keeps on giving, because the Giver it reveals is inexhaustible in His love and grace.

Tragically, though, fewer and fewer people, even those who number themselves among God's everlasting family, are opening this gift and seeking to understand what it's all about and how to use it. They often feel intimidated by it. It requires some assembly, and its instructions are hard to comprehend sometimes. How does the Bible fit together anyway?

What does Genesis have to do with Revelation? Who are Abraham and Moses, and what is their relationship to Jesus and Paul? And what about the works of the Law and the works of faith? What are they all about, and how do they fit together, if at all?

And what does this ancient Book have to say to us who are looking toward the twenty-first century? Will taking the time and energy to understand its instructions and to fit it all together really help you and me? Will it help us better understand who we are, what the future holds, how we can better live here and now? Will it really help us in our personal relationships, in our marriages and families, in our jobs? Can it give us more than just advice on how to handle crises? the death of a loved one? the financial fallout of losing a job? catastrophic illness? betrayal by a friend? the seduction of our values? the abuses of the heart and soul? Will it allay our fears and calm our restlessness and heal our wounds? Can it really get us in touch with the same power that gave birth to the universe? that parted the Red Sea? that raised Jesus from the stranglehold of the grave? Can we really find unconditional love, total forgiveness, and genuine healing in its pages?

Yes. Yes. Without a shred of doubt.

The *Spirit-Filled Life Bible Discovery Guide* series is designed to help you unwrap, assemble, and enjoy all God has for you in the pages of Scripture. It will focus your time and energy on the books of the Bible, the people and places they describe, and the themes and life applications that flow thick from its pages like honey oozing from a beehive.

So you can get the most out of God's Word, this series has a number of helpful features. Each study guide has no more than fourteen lessons, each arranged so you can plumb the depths or skim the surface, depending on your needs and interests.

The study guides also contain six major sections, each marked by a symbol and heading for easy identification.

WORD WEALTH

The WORD WEALTH feature provides important definitions of key terms.

BEHIND THE SCENES

BEHIND THE SCENES supplies information about cultural beliefs and practices, doctrinal disputes, business trades, and the like, that illuminate Bible passages and teachings.

AT A GLANCE

The AT A GLANCE feature uses maps and charts to identify places and simplify themes or positions.

BIBLE EXTRA

Because this study guide focuses on a book of the Bible, you will find a BIBLE EXTRA feature that guides you into Bible dictionaries, Bible encyclopedias, and other resources that will enable you to glean more from the Bible's wealth if you want something extra.

PROBING THE DEPTHS

Another feature, PROBING THE DEPTHS, will explain controversial issues raised by particular lessons and cite Bible passages and other sources to which you can turn to help you come to your own conclusions.

FAITH ALIVE

Finally, each lesson contains a FAITH ALIVE feature. Here the focus is, So what? Given what the Bible says, what does it mean for my life? How can it impact my day-to-day needs, hurts, relationships, concerns, and whatever else is important to me? FAITH ALIVE will help you see and apply the practical relevance of God's literary gift.

As you'll see, these guides supply space for you to answer the study and life-application questions and exercises. You may, however, want to record all your answers, or just the overflow from your study or application, in a separate notebook or journal. This would be especially helpful if you think you'll dig into the BIBLE EXTRA features. Because the exercises in this feature are optional and can be expanded as far as you want to take them, we have not allowed writing space for them in this study guide. So you may want to have a notebook or journal handy for recording your discoveries while working through to this feature's riches.

The Bible study method used in this series revolves around four basic steps: observation, interpretation, correlation, and application. Observation answers the question, What does the text say? Interpretation deals with, What does the text mean?—not with what it means to you or me, but what it meant to its original readers. Correlation asks, What light do other Scripture passages shed on this text? And application, the goal of Bible study, poses the question, How should my life change in response to the Holy Spirit's teaching of this text?

If you have used a Bible much before, you know that it comes in a variety of translations and paraphrases. Although you can use any of them with profit as you work through the *Spirit-Filled Life Bible Discovery Guide* series, when Bible passages or words are cited, you will find they are from the New King James Version of the Bible. Using this translation with this series will make your study easier, but it's certainly not necessary.

The only resources you need to complete and apply these study guides are a heart and mind open to the Holy Spirit, a prayerful attitude, and a pencil and a Bible. Of course, you may draw upon other sources, such as commentaries, dictionaries, encyclopedias, atlases, and concordances, and you'll even find some optional exercises that will guide you into these sources. But these are extras, not necessities. These study guides are comprehensive enough to give you all you need to gain a good, basic understanding of the Bible book being covered and how you can apply its themes and counsel to your life.

A word of warning, though. By itself, Bible study will not transform your life. It will not give you power, peace, joy, comfort, hope, and a number of other gifts God longs for you to unwrap and enjoy. Through Bible study, you will grow in your understanding of the Lord, His kingdom and your place in it, and those things are essential. But you need more. You need to rely on the Holy Spirit to guide your study and your application of the Bible's truths. He, Jesus promised, was sent to teach us "all things" (John 14:26; cf. 1 Cor. 2:13). So as you use this series to guide you through Scripture, bathe your study time in prayer, asking the Spirit of God to illuminate the text, enlighten your mind, humble your will, and comfort your heart. He will never let you down.

My prayer and goal for you is that as you unwrap and begin to explore God's Book for living His way, the Holy Spirit will fill every fiber of your being with the joy and power God longs to give all His children. So read on. Be diligent. Stay open and submissive to Him. You will not be disappointed. He promises you!

Lesson 1/The Best Revelation (1:1—2:4)

Errol Flynn swashbuckled his way through a Hollywood version of *The Adventures of Robin Hood* in 1938. In that film, the part of Little John was played by a fine actor named Alan Hale. Hale's Little John was a jolly version of Robin's husky sidekick, but unfortunately you can't picture him because Alan Hale is unfamiliar to most people today.

Wait a minute. Yes, you can picture Alan Hale's Little John because you know what his son looks like, and Alan Hale, Jr., is the spitting image of his father. Picture the Skipper from "Gilligan's Island." Do you have him in your mind's eye? Dress the Skipper in Sherwood Forest garb and you have Alan Hale's Little John—same build, same smile, same face and hair. Like father; like son.

Do you want to know what God is like? No one has ever seen Him; in fact, no one can look at God and live. However, God sent His Son into the world to make a sacrifice for the sins of mankind. In the time Jesus lived on earth He demonstrated exactly what His Father is like. Then when the apostles explained the life and ministry of Jesus in the New Testament writings, they further clarified what the Father is like. The Epistle to the Hebrews begins with this important idea about revelation.

THE BIG PICTURE

The Epistle to the Hebrews is about Christ in His glory. The writer pulls together key insights about Jesus and His life on earth with a number of theological conclusions from the Old Testament concerning the preincarnate Christ and the ministry of Christ in glory today. The few but important references to Jesus "in the days of His flesh" (Heb. 5:7) help us trust Him as one who intimately knows our human frailties, yet is not ashamed to call us His brothers (Heb. 2:11)! The abundant Old Testament quotations and arguments portray Jesus as Son greater than Moses, the conqueror greater than Joshua, and the priest greater than Aaron. In all respects, Christ supersedes all! And His present ministry as intercessor for believers assures us that we shall persevere until we fully receive the "kingdom which cannot be shaken" (Heb. 11:28).

Look up the following representative passages from each major portion of Hebrews and summarize their contents.

I. The Ways Christ is Superior (Heb. 1:1—4:13)

Hebrews 2:5-9

II. The Superiority of Christ's Works (Heb. 4:14—10:18)

Hebrews 10:11-18

III. The Superiority of the Walk of Faith (Heb. 10:19—13:25)

Hebrews 12:1-4

An astonishing characteristic of the Epistle to the Hebrews is a series of stern warnings that sometimes leave readers quaking in their spiritual boots. Summarize these warnings. *Warn @ drifting away*

Hebrews 2:1-4

Hebrews 3:12–15

Hebrews 10:26–31

Hebrews 12:25–29

Although the writer of Hebrews issued such stern warnings to his readers, what was his basic attitude toward them? (Heb. 6:9, 10)

What did the author pray for those who read his book? (Heb. 13:20, 21)

EVERYTHING YOU EVER WANTED TO KNOW ABOUT GOD

BEHIND THE SCENES

The author of the Epistle to the Hebrews is anonymous. The King James Version attributed the epistle to Paul, and some interpreters support this tradition. Because the Greek style is more classical than Paul's, other interpreters hypothesize that Paul wrote the epistle originally in Aramaic and that Luke translated it into Greek for a more general audience.

Still others reason from the polished style that the orator Apollos wrote Hebrews (see Acts 18:24–28). Priscilla is the candidate for authorship favored by some who suggest that a woman would have had reason to remain anonymous in first century Jewish and Christian culture. Barnabas also has his supporters in the Who-Wrote-Hebrews Derby. Origen in the third century stated that "only God knows for certain who wrote Hebrews."

The writer to the Hebrews stressed throughout his letter that everything about the New Covenant in Christ is superior to the Old Covenant of the Mosaic Law. The first two verses of chapter one sets the tone for this line of thought as the author compares the work of God in revealing the Old and New Testaments.

From Hebrews 1:1, 2 complete the following comparative chart about the revelation of the Old and New Testaments.

	OLD TESTAMENT	NEW TESTAMENT
Source		
Verb of revelation		
Time		
Agent		
Completeness		

 WORD WEALTH

"At various times and in various ways" translates the Greek phrase *polumeros kai polutropos.* You don't have to know a word of Greek to see that these two adverbs were carefully chosen because they look alike and would sound alike. This poetic touch can't be captured in English. We have to use longer expressions like "every now and then" and "here a little, there a little."

What is said about the Son in Hebrews 1:2, 3 relative to each of these topics?

His relationship to God

His relationship to all of creation

His relationship to human creation

What conclusions do you think the author of Hebrews expected his readers to draw about God's self-revelation in His Son from 1:1–3?

FAITH ALIVE

Which idea(s) in Hebrews 1:1–3 about the Son of God impress(es) you most? Why?

What do you know about God because His Son showed it in His life that you couldn't know otherwise?

HEAD AND SHOULDERS ABOVE ANYTHING ELSE

In both Hebrew and Greek the words translated "angel" meant "messenger." The author of Hebrews opened his epistle with an assertion that the Son was the greatest messenger about God. The balance of chapter 1 expands on the superiority of the Son to the angelic messengers.

BEHIND THE SCENES

Although angels are not mentioned in Exodus at the time when God delivered the Law to Moses on Mount Sinai, Judaism in the New Testament era understood that God used angels in some fashion as intermediaries in the transmission of the Law. The Greek translation of the Old Testament in Deuteronomy 33:2 said multitudes of angels (rather than "saints") accompanied God to Mount Sinai. The martyr Stephen in Acts 7:53 and the Apostle Paul in Galatians 3:19 add New Testament confirmation that angels were involved in the giving of the Mosaic Law. The writer to the Hebrews makes it clear that the Son is a vastly better Messenger than the next best ones.

What is the first evidence that the Son is superior to the angels? (Heb. 1:4)

WORD WEALTH

The basic theme of Hebrews is found in the word *better*, describing the superiority of Christ in His person and work (1:4; 6:9; 7:7, 19, 22; 8:6; 9:23; 10:34; 11:16, 35, 40; 12:24). The words *perfect* and *heavenly* are also prominent. Christ offers a better revelation, position, priesthood, covenant, sacrifice, and power. The writer develops this theme to prevent the readers from giving up the substance for the shadow by abandoning Christianity and retreating into the old Jewish system. This epistle is also written to exhort them to become mature in Christ and to put away their spiritual dullness and degeneration. Thus, it stresses doctrine, particularly Christology (the study of Christ) and soteriology (the study of salvation).[1]

In Hebrews 1:5, 6 what contrast between the Son and the angels did the writer establish by quoting Psalm 2:7; 2 Samuel

7:14; and Deuteronomy 32:43 (from the Greek Old Testament)?

In Hebrews 1:7–9 what contrast between the Son and the angels did the writer establish by quoting Psalm 104:4 and Psalm 45:6, 7?

In Hebrews 1:10–12 what implied contrast between the Son and the angels did the writer establish by quoting Psalm 102:25–27?

In Hebrews 1:13, 14 what contrast between the Son and the angels did the writer establish by quoting Psalm 110:1?

BEHIND THE SCENES

Ministering Spirits (Heb. 1:14). Surprisingly enough, there are more direct references to angels in the New Testament than in the Old Testament. A careful study will reveal that the New Testament activity of angels usually revolves around the ministry of Jesus and the establishment of His church on earth. They "minister" (Greek *diakonia*), referring to their "serviceable labor, assistance." They are ministering spirits, or heavenly assistants, who are continually active today in building the body of Christ—advancing the ministry of Jesus and the building of His church.[2]

BIBLE EXTRA

Look up each of the Old Testament quotations utilized in Hebrews 1:5–14. Compare the meaning of each passage in its context with the way the writer to the Hebrews used it.

Psalm 2:7 (Old Testament meaning)

(meaning in Hebrews)

2 Samuel 7:14 (Old Testament meaning)

(meaning in Hebrews)

Because the Deuteronomy 32:43 quotation is from a portion of the Greek Old Testament not found in the Hebrew Old Testament, compare the similar passage in Psalm 97:7.

Psalm 97:7 (Old Testament meaning)

(meaning in Hebrews)

Psalm 104:4 (Old Testament meaning)

(meaning in Hebrews)

Psalm 45:6, 7 (Old Testament meaning)

(meaning in Hebrews)

Psalm 102:25–27 (Old Testament meaning)

(meaning in Hebrews)

Psalm 110:1 (Old Testament meaning)

(meaning in Hebrews)

 ## FAITH ALIVE

Write a prayer of praise to Christ based on His characteristics described in the Old Testament quotations found in Hebrews 1:5–14.

What ministry would you like to receive from the angels of God in your life and church?

GREAT PRIVILEGE CARRIES GREAT RESPONSIBILITY

The writer to the Hebrews ventures far into the theological significance of the Old Testament and the person of the

Son of God, but he never loses sight of the practical significance of learning spiritual truth. In Hebrews 2:1–4, the author
issues the first of five stern warnings for his readers to act on
the truth that they have received (see 4:1–3, 11–13; 5:12—
6:12; 10:19–39; 12:12–29).

What is the danger inherent in paying insufficient attention to divine revelation? (Heb. 2:1)

How did God respond to transgression of His Old
Covenant with Israel? (Heb. 2:2)

What role did each of these play in bringing the "great
salvation" to the Hebrews? (Heb. 2:3, 4)

The Lord (Jesus)

Those who heard Him (the apostles)

God

BEHIND THE SCENES

The author argues from the lesser to the greater. If disobedience to a revelation transmitted by angels was severely
punished, indifference to the salvation brought by Christ
receives even greater punishment. The greatness of salvation
is confirmed by three facts: it was spoken by the Lord; it was
confirmed by the apostles; it was attested by the ministry of
the Holy Spirit through miracles and spiritual gifts (see 1 Cor.
12:8–11). It is an age-long expectation that such manifesta-
tions of Christ's glory will be ministered by the Holy Spirit in
confirming the spread of the gospel (Mark 16:20; 1 Cor. 2:4).[3]

FAITH ALIVE

Why do you think the writer to the Hebrews did not spell out the consequences of neglecting "so great a salvation" [2:3] when he had mentioned the scrupulous judgment attached to breaking the Law?

What kind of response do you think the author wanted from the Hebrews to his warning in 2:1–4?

What kind of emotional reaction did you have to this first warning?

If you felt fear in response to this warning, look at Hebrews 2:14–18 and 1 John 4:17–19. Read Hebrews 6:9–12. What does the writer to the Hebrews say is the purpose of his stern warnings?

1. "Keys to Hebrews," *The New Open Bible: NKJV* (Nashville: Thomas Nelson Publishers, 1990), 1447.
2. *Spirit-Filled Life Bible* (Nashville: Thomas Nelson Publishers, 1991), 1873, "Kingdom Dynamics: Heb. 1:14, Ministering Spirits."
3. Ibid., note on Hebrews 2:3, 4.

Lesson 2/The Best Man
(2:5–18)

During the winter of 1777–78 the Continental Army of the rebelling American colonies shivered in Valley Forge while the British forces occupied and rested in Philadelphia. Conditions at Valley Forge were so miserable and supplies so inadequate that the desertion rate from the ranks of the Continentals exceeded the rate of arrival by new recruits.

The only reason the Continental Army survived at Valley Forge was because George Washington was with it. The impression Washington's character had made on his men through months of service together inspired enough loyalty to keep the Continental Army intact and the British army bottled up.

Washington suffered with his men. He endured their privations and continually interceded with the Continental Congress for provisions and supplies. The troops in the huts who lacked boots, blankets, and food knew the General was their fellow-sufferer and champion with the powers-that-be.

Washington had come out of retirement to lead the Continental forces, and once the Revolution was successfully completed he tried to retreat once more to the beauty of Mount Vernon.

MAN OF DESTINY

The Epistle to the Hebrews opened with grand assertions about the deity of the Son of God, His role in sustaining all of creation, and His superiority over the angels as the Revealer of the Father to humanity. This paean of praise set the stage for the main idea the writer of Hebrews wanted to express about the Son. This awesome Being has shared human nature and experience so fully that He is both Jesus the Man and Jesus the Son of God. The author of Hebrews emphasizes the genuine humanity of Jesus as well as Christ's deity. It was this unique combination of humanity and deity that enabled Him to be both our Savior and our High Priest. Hebrews 4:15 states, "For we do not have a High Priest who cannot sympathize with our weaknesses, but was in all points tempted as we are, yet without sin."

What three-way contrast between the angels, humans, and the Son did the writer of Hebrews make in 2:5–9?

BEHIND THE SCENES

Angels are an order of heavenly beings superior to humans in power and intelligence. By nature angels are spiritual (Heb. 1:14) and superior to human nature (2:7), and they have superhuman power and knowledge (2 Sam. 14:17, 20; 2 Pet. 2:11). They are not, however, all-powerful and all-knowing (Ps. 103:20; 2 Thess. 1:7).

Angels were created by God (Ps. 148:2, 5) and were present to rejoice when He created the world (Job 38:4–7). In their original state they were holy, but before the creation of the world, some of them rebelled against God and lost this exalted position.

Unfallen angels are known for their reverence for God and their obedience to His will. Angels represent God in announcing good news (Gen. 18:9, 10; Luke 1:13, 30; 2:8–15). On His behalf they also warn of coming dangers (Gen. 18:16—19:29; Matt. 2:13). In some cases they are God's agents in the destruction and judgment of evil (Gen. 19:13; 2 Sam. 24:16). They also were particularly active in the events surrounding the birth and resurrection of Jesus (Matt. 1:20; 2:13, 19; 28:2; Luke 1:11–38; 2:9–15; 22:43; 24:23; John 20:12).

Although they are not the objects of salvation, angels are interested in the salvation of human beings (Luke 15:10; 1 Cor. 4:9).[1]

What did the writer of Hebrews observe about the dominion of man over creation that David wrote about in Psalm 8? (Heb. 2:8)

What does the death of Jesus have to do with the dominion of mankind? (Heb. 2:9)

Prior to Hebrews 2:9, the writer of Hebrews consistently used the title "the Son." Why do you think he introduced the name "Jesus" at this point? Why not use it earlier?

According to Hebrews 2:7, when was Jesus "made a little lower than the angels"? (2:9)

How do you think Jesus was "crowned with glory and honor"? (Heb. 2:9)

 BEHIND THE SCENES

God has purposed men and not angels to be sovereigns of the created order. "The world to come" (v. 5) is the new eternal order inaugurated by the enthronement of Christ which is to be consummated at His return.

Instead of assuming his intended dominion over creation, man had become a slave, held in bondage by death and Satan.

So the eternal Son of God appeared in history on Earth as Jesus the Man to provide a way of escape from bondage, access to God's presence, and an entrance into man's intended glory. Jesus the Man, exalted in glory at God's right hand, occupies the position of dominion intended for men, with everything put, or to be put, in subjection under his feet (v. 8).[2]

 FAITH ALIVE

Compare Genesis 1:27, 28; Hebrews 1:2, 3; and 2:1–9. How is Jesus equipped to repair the damage done by sin to the image of God within your personality?

In what way(s) do you think that humans, who are created for dominion (Heb. 2:7, 8), are temporarily lower than the angels, who are created to be servants? (Heb. 1:14)

How is man God's unique creation, and what is the eternal destiny of those who are "joint heirs" with Jesus Christ? (Eph. 1:18; 2:6)

MAN OF SOLIDARITY

The writer of Hebrews extended the idea that Jesus was able to be our High Priest because He "was in all points tempted as we are, yet without sin" (Heb. 4:15). Jesus Christ is able to identify with our weaknesses completely because, when He was on earth, He was tempted with the same sins we face in our daily lives. When we exercise our faith in Jesus Christ to overcome the power of sin and temptation in our lives, we may be confident that God's greater power, as well as

His patient compassion, flow to us through Jesus Christ. In short, God has walked where we walk and lived where we live, and, through the presence of Jesus, He still does.

Hebrews 2:9 introduced the idea that God graciously sent His Son Jesus to die for mankind. In verses 10 and 11, how is this idea expanded with regard to all three participants?

God

Jesus

Mankind

WORD WEALTH

"**Captain** of their salvation." The Greek word does not translate easily into English. The NKJV translation "captain" emphasizes supremacy. The NRSV translation "pioneer" captures the idea of participation. The NIV translation "author" develops the idea of origination. Jesus originated salvation; He is the supreme Savior; and He gets personally involved with those being saved. The context of Hebrews 2 stresses the participatory aspect of the term.

Jesus Christ was the eternal Son of God Incarnate as a man—fully God and also fully and sinlessly human. The Father caused the Son to live for thirty-some years and die a shameful death so that He would be perfect, in the sense of completed, as a Sanctifier (Heb. 2:10). How do you think Jesus' life and death prepared Him to guide Christians into holiness?

Why is Jesus not ashamed to call those being sanctified His brothers? (Heb. 2:11)

How do you think the quotations from Psalm 22:22 and Isaiah 8:17 and 18 support the author's contention that Jesus gladly identified Christians as His brothers? (Look up the Old Testament passages in their contexts for further insight.)

Psalm 22:22

Isaiah 8:17

Isaiah 8:18

BEHIND THE SCENES

Praise Releases the Spirit of Prophecy (Heb. 2:11, 12). This text quotes the messianic prophecy in Psalm 22:22, showing how the Spirit of the Christ fills the New Testament church, and how Christ identifies Himself so closely with His people when they sing praises. As they do, two important things happen: 1) He joins in the song Himself, and 2) this praise releases the spirit of prophecy. The latter is in the words *"I will declare your name to My brethren."*

As we joyfully sing praise to our God, Christ comes to flood our minds with the glory of the Father's character ("name"). There is no doubt about it—the praises of the people in the church service release the spirit of prophetic revelation—the magnifying of God through Jesus Christ. Thus, praise introduces edification, exhortation, and comfort to bless the whole body.[3]

FAITH ALIVE

What is your response to the direct biblical statement that Jesus willingly calls you His brother or sister?

Both the context of Hebrews 2 and the contexts of the Old Testament quotations concern affliction and suffering. How can you find help in times of distress from the knowledge that Jesus stands in solidarity with you in that distress?

MAN OF LIBERTY

Jesus the perfect Man stood solidly alongside all humans. But He didn't become a man and suffer just to be an example that inspires and motivates people to live better lives. The suffering and death of Jesus was much more than an example. His death was a redemptive act that set believing people free from the power of sin and death.

What characteristics of humanity did the writer of Hebrews represent by the expression "flesh and blood"? (2:14)

In what sense do you think that Satan had the power of death? (Heb. 2:14, 15)

In what sense did Jesus destroy the Devil and his use of the fear of death? (Heb. 2:14, 15)

BEHIND THE SCENES

The devil is the main title for the angelic being who is the supreme enemy of God and man. Satan is his name, and devil is what he is—the accuser or deceiver. The title "devil" appears 35 times in the NKJV. In every case it is preceded by the article "the," indicating a title rather than a name. The term comes from a Greek word that means "a false witness" or "malicious accuser."

The devil is man's worst enemy (Matt. 13:25, 28, 38). This is the one enemy Jesus does not want us to love. He is an enemy of Christ, the church, and the gospel; and he is tireless in his efforts to uproot good and sow evil.

"He was a murderer from the beginning" (John 8:44) are the strong words from the lips of Jesus. The devil killed Abel and the prophets, and he wanted to kill Jesus before His time (8:40).

Starting with Eve, the devil has attempted to deceive every living soul (Rev. 20:10). Evil men operating under the power of the Evil One will continue to deceive (2 Tim. 3:13).

Three times Jesus called the devil "the ruler of this world" (John 12:31; 14:30; 16:11). The devil offered the world to Jesus if He would worship him (Luke 4:5–7), but the Lord refused with these words, "Get behind Me, Satan" (4:8). At Calvary God dealt a death blow to this world ruler. It is only a matter of time before God will win the final victory at the end of time (1 John 3:8; Matt. 25:41; Rev. 12:7).

The devil is strong, but Christians are stronger through the Lord (Eph. 6:11). The devil tempts, but God provides a way of escape (1 Cor. 10:13); the devil tries to take advantage of people (2 Cor. 2:11), but he will flee if fought (James 4:7). The devil should not be feared, for Jesus is more powerful than this deceiving prince of the demons (1 John 4:4).[4]

Why would it have been insufficient for the Son of God to enter human history as an angel (or any form other than a truly human one)? (Heb. 2:16, 17)

According to Hebrews 2:17 and 18, what has Jesus done as a High Priest relative to these two sin problems?

The penalty for sin

The temptation to sin

WORD WEALTH

"**To make propitiation** for the sins of the people" (Heb. 2:17). "To propitiate" means to satisfy the wrath of God which has been justly and necessarily provoked by sin. It's a complicated concept that implies, on the one hand, that God's righteous wrath was directed against Jesus as the substitute for sinful people. On the other hand, propitiation requires the justification of those whose sins have been forgiven. Forgiven sinners must be given the righteousness of Jesus so that they can stand in the presence of God in His holiness. Propitiation does not change God's standards; it changes people to meet His standards.

What do mercy and faithfulness on Jesus' part as High Priest have to do with propitiation and help against temptation? (Heb. 2:17, 18)

FAITH ALIVE

Hebrews 2:18 says that Jesus "suffered, being tempted" and, on that basis, is able to sympathetically help you with your temptations. Do you think that the temptations that Jesus experienced during His lifetime had much appeal to Him?

How powerful did His temptations have to be before you think His experience would help Him understand your temptations?

What encouragement do you gain from knowing that Jesus became a perfect human being in order to die for sin?

What encouragement do you gain from knowing that Jesus gladly calls all Christians His brothers?

What encouragement do you gain from knowing that Jesus sets you free from sin and death?

1. "Angel," *Nelson's Illustrated Bible Dictionary* (Nashville: Thomas Nelson Publishers, 1986), 47–48.

2. *Spirit-Filled Life Bible* (Nashville: Thomas Nelson Publishers, 1991), 1873, 1874, notes on Hebrews 2:5–9 and Hebrews 2:8, 9.

3. Ibid., 1874, "Kingdom Dynamics: Hebrews 2:11, 12, Praise Releases the Spirit of Prophecy."

4. "Devil," *Nelson's Illustrated Bible Dictionary*, 299–300.

Lesson 3/The Best Hope for Peace with God (3:1—4:13)

Pastor Smith looked across his desk at Mrs. Jones and wondered what to do next. Several weeks had gone by in this pastoral counseling situation and they were at an impasse. This poor woman had come to him depressed and exhausted from trying to cope with an impossible burden of bitterness and anger. Now it seemed that she couldn't let go of this burden. The resentment was destroying her, but it was a familiar companion of many years.

Mrs. Jones had wept to tell of the betrayal she had experienced as a child at the hand of her parents, as a young woman at the hand of her husband, and as a middle-aged adult at the hands of her grown children. Everybody owed her an emotional debt. She seemed to have a library of videotaped scenes from her past in which people important to her wounded her. Life was too much for her because of the burden of her memories.

Pastor Smith had talked with Mrs. Jones about Jesus Christ and forgiveness, and she professed to trust Christ as her Savior. When he talked with her about the need to forgive others as Christ forgave her, she reluctantly agreed. When they discussed the relationship between granting forgiveness to others and enjoying the forgiveness provided in Christ, Mrs. Jones grew uncomfortable.

For two weeks Pastor Smith had realized that they had been marking time. He said to her, "We aren't making much progress these days."

"No," she replied, "you keep giving me these dumb little Bible verses to look at that don't have anything to do with my situation."

"Why do you think they don't have anything to do with you?"

"You act like God wants me to let everyone hurt me, and I won't do it. They've hurt me, and I'm not going to let them get away with it."

And Mrs. Jones left without any of the peace she had said earlier that she wanted.

THE BEST PERSONAL SAVIOR

Mrs. Jones wanted peace as a result of the humiliation of all of her perceived enemies. The writer of Hebrews envisioned peace, or "rest," as a matter of relationship with God. He reasoned with his Hebrew Christian readers that Christ Jesus was the key to peace with God. Hebrews 2 concluded with reference to Jesus as the perfect Priest for fallen people because of the temptations and sufferings He experienced in His incarnate state. Chapter 3 picks up right at that idea.

What has been said about Jesus in Hebrews 1—2 that would justify calling His followers by the unusual names "holy brethren, partakers of the heavenly calling"? (Heb. 3:1)

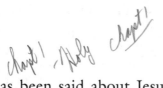

What has been said about Jesus in Hebrews 1—2 that would justify calling Him "the Apostle [the Commissioned One] . . . of our confession"? (Heb. 3:1)

What has been said about Jesus in Hebrews 1—2 that would justify calling Him "the High Priest [Intercessor on behalf of sins] of our confession"? (Heb. 3:1)

          WORD WEALTH

Confession has two primary senses in the New Testament, both of them springing out of the root idea of agreement or saying the same thing about an issue. One New Testament usage of "confession" pertains to penitence for sin. One who confesses sin agrees with God that it is evil.

The second New Testament usage of "confession" pertains to agreeing with the faith, saying the same thing that all other believers in Jesus Christ say about Him. In this sense "confession" is close in meaning to "witness" and "proclamation."

What do you suppose the Hebrew Christians had confessed about Christ Jesus? (Heb. 3:1; 4:14; 10:23)

In what matters did the writer of Hebrews affirm that Jesus and Moses were alike? (Heb. 3:2–6)

In what matters did the writer of Hebrews affirm that Jesus was superior to Moses? (Heb. 3:2–6)

Over what house was Moses faithful in the Old Testament? (Heb. 3:2, 5; Num. 12:7)

Over what house was Jesus faithful in the New Testament? (Heb. 3:6; 1 Pet. 2:5)

Why was Christ Jesus of greater glory and honor than Moses in the household of God? (Heb. 3:1–3)

 BEHIND THE SCENES

The writer of Hebrews extended his discussion of the superiority of the revelation of God in Christ to include Moses, the lawgiver, who was revered by Israel as the greatest man who ever lived. Earlier the author had demonstrated that Jesus was superior to the angels who mediated the Law. Now he focused on the superiority of Jesus as the receiver and recorder of the Law.

Moses was the Hebrew prophet who delivered the Israelites from Egyptian slavery and who was their leader and lawgiver during their years of wandering in the wilderness. Moses was a leader so inspired by God that he was able to build a united nation from a race of oppressed and weary slaves. In the covenant ceremony at Mount Sinai, where the Ten Commandments were given, he founded the religious community known as Israel. As the interpreter of these covenant laws, he was the organizer of the community's religious and civil traditions. His story is told in the Old Testament—in the books of Exodus, Leviticus, Numbers, and Deuteronomy.

After his death, Moses continued to be viewed by Israel as the servant of the Lord (Josh. 1:1, 2) and as the one through whom God spoke to Israel (Josh. 1:3; 8:24; 14:2). For that reason, although it was truly the Law of God, the Law given at Mount Sinai was consistently called the Law of Moses (Josh. 1:7, 4:10).

The writer Hebrews spoke in glowing terms of the faith of Moses (Heb. 11:24–29). These and other passages demonstrate how highly Moses was esteemed by various writers of the Old and New Testaments.

The New Testament, however, shows that Moses' teaching was intended only to prepare humanity for the greater teaching and work of Jesus Christ (Rom. 1:16—3:31). What Moses promised, Jesus fulfilled: "For the law was given through Moses, but grace and truth came through Jesus Christ" (John 1:17).[1]

What was Moses' function in God's household? (Heb. 3:5)

What is Christ Jesus' function in the household of God? (Heb. 3:6)

What do you think is the relation between the confession of the readers in Hebrews 3:1 and their holding fast in verse 6? (see v. 14)

What progression of steps on the part of Israel's wandering in the wilderness led to chastening by God? (Heb. 3:16–19)

What progression of reactions did God have to the unbelief of Israel in the wilderness? (Heb. 3:17–19)

What all do you think is involved in the spiritual concept "unbelief" that provokes the patience, mercy, and love of God? (Heb. 3:19)

 BEHIND THE SCENES

The wanderings of Israel include the activities of the Israelite tribes during the period between their departure from Egypt under Moses and the time when they were encamped by the Jordan River, ready to be led into Canaan by Joshua. The period of time covered by these events is traditionally 40 years, much of which was spent in the area of Kadesh-Barnea.

The Israelite journeyings are commonly spoken of as "wilderness wanderings," because they took the people through some areas that were known as wilderness. Although a wilderness may have desert areas, it has grassy upland plains, oasis springs, and vegetation, such as flowers, shurbs, and trees that can support a surprising variety of animal life.

At Mount Sinai, Israel received the Law and settled for nearly a year (Num. 1:1; 10:11) while Moses worked at organizing the new nation. At this stage of the wanderings, the construction of the tabernacle and the regulations governing its use were given careful attention because of their importance for the future life of the Israelites.

Even these precautions, however, were not enough to stop dissatisfaction among the wandering Israelites as they traveled toward Kadesh. The people complained about the lack of food in the wilderness. Even when God provided manna, they soon began to dislike it.

Eventually the people refused to enter Canaan and rebelled against their leaders. God was angry with them. With the exception of Joshua and Caleb, all the people alive at that time were condemned to spend the rest of their lives in the wilderness.[2]

FAITH ALIVE

What does it mean to you to be part of the "house" which by inheritance belongs to Jesus? How should you feel and act because of that status?

THE BEST PERSONAL EXAMPLE

Mrs. Jones wanted peace at the expense of everyone around her. She could not bring herself to trust God through a painful process of forgiveness. The writer of Hebrews said peace begins with a relationship with God through Jesus Christ. That relationship expresses itself in faith and perseverance. He illustrated the necessity of enduring faith by exposing the lack of it in the history of Israel during the wilderness wanderings before they entered the Promised Land.

The Epistle to the Hebrews began with God as the Revealer (1:1) and His Son as the ultimate means of revelation

(v. 2). The Son's human name, Jesus, figured prominently in the second chapter (v. 9) to stress His identification with all humans. Finally in chapter 3, the Holy Spirit makes His appearance. What is the role of the Holy Spirit in Hebrews 3:7–11?

BEHIND THE SCENES

The writer testifies to the inspiration of the Old Testament by ascribing the quote from Psalm 95 to the Holy Spirit. Using the tragic failure of the Israelites in the wilderness as an example, he solemnly warns his readers of the peril of unbelief (see 1 Cor. 10:11). Their spirit of disobedience resulted in God's wrath, excluding them from entrance into the promised rest of Canaan (v. 11).[3]

What was the failure of faith on the part of the Israelites during their forty years of wandering in the wilderness as recorded in Psalm 95:7–11 and quoted in Hebrews 3:7–11?

WORD WEALTH

Rest is an important term in this section of Hebrews. Circle all of the occurrences of "rest" in the section from Hebrews 3:11 to 4:11. How many times did "rest" appear? _____ The Greek word in Hebrews has a prefix that suggests causation. The freedom from stress and effort in the root of the noun depends on an external cause—in this case upon God who gives or withholds the "rest" (3:11, 18; 4:1, 3, 5, 10).

The Hebrew term for "rest" in Psalm 95 contains the idea of soothing comfort. In Psalm 23:2, the divine Shepherd leads beside waters of "rest." The name Noah, meaning a place of sanctuary, derives from this noun.

What conclusion did the writer of Hebrews draw from his quotation of Psalm 95? (Heb. 3:12–15)

What seem to be the components of the kind of unbelief that the writer to the Hebrews warned against? (Heb. 3:7–19)

What action did the writer urge the Hebrew Christians to take against "an evil heart of unbelief"? (Heb. 3:12, 13)

Compare the spiritual danger warned against in Hebrews 2:3 with the one warned against in 3:12, 13.

FAITH ALIVE

From the two warnings in Hebrews 2 and 3, what would you conclude was the major concern the writer of the epistle had about his readers?

Was the writer trying to frighten or encourage his readers? How did you reach your conclusion?

What kind of witness does the Holy Spirit bear with your spirit through the warning of Hebrews 3?

THE BEST PERSONAL PROMISE

Mrs. Jones clung to her grudges and dreams of revenge. She would not let go of them long enough to examine the promises of peace in God's Word. They were silly Bible verses in comparison to the reality of the knots of pain her spirit was tied into. She hated the pain, but she was accustomed to it. It was a familiar if unpleasant companion. There was too much risk involved in giving up the familiar pain for the unfamiliar promise of peace and rest.

What determines whether someone who hears the gospel actually enters God's rest? (Heb. 4:1–3)

BEHIND THE SCENES

Faith believes what God says and acts in line with His Word. Faith allows the believer to enter the rest into which God has called all His people. It acknowledges the completed work of salvation, while faithfully obeying every instruction from God.

Enter the rest promised by God. **Mix** your faith with God's Word. **Do not allow** rebellion to harden your heart. **Devote your whole heart** to obeying God and His Word. **Trust** Him to do the things He says He will do.[4]

How did the writer of Hebrews reason from the Old Testament that someone other than Israel had to enter God's rest? (Heb. 4:3–9)

How does the idea of God's Sabbath rest from Creation give meaning to the rest belonging to the people of God? (Heb. 4:4, 9)

BEHIND THE SCENES

Israel's failure to enter Canaan becomes a solemn warning, lest professing Christians fail to enter the rest that God has promised. This rest is not entrance to Canaan, as it is in Hebrews 3:18, but that historical event is a type of the rest to be enjoyed by Christians. Some commentators view rest as a future heavenly rest, while others feel that the term describes the present experience of the believer who has fully surrendered to the lordship of Christ and is totally controlled by the Holy Spirit.[5]

Do you think the rest that exists for the people of God spoken of in Hebrews 3—4 is primarily a reference to the eternal state of redeemed humanity or primarily a reference to the quality of life "the Apostle and High Priest of our confession, Christ Jesus" (3:1) intends for Christians in this life? Why?

Examine Hebrews 3:12, 13 and 4:11 for appropriate steps to take in order to enter into God's rest. Condense them into a single sentence of spiritual advice.

What does God's Word reveal to Him about people? (Heb. 4.12, 13)

BEHIND THE SCENES

The term for "word" here is the Greek word *logos,* which commonly indicates the expression of a complete idea and is used in referring to the Holy Scriptures. It contrasts with *rhema,* which generally refers to a word spoken or given. This recommends to our understanding the difference between *all* the Bible and the *single* promise or promises the Holy Spirit may bring to our mind from the Word of God.

When facing a situation of need, trial, or difficulty, the promises of God may become a *rhema* to you; that is, a weapon of the Spirit, "the word of God" (Eph. 6:17). Its authority is that this "word" comes from the Bible—God's

Word—the completed *logos*. Its immediate significance is that He has "spoken" it to your soul by His Spirit and is calling forth faith just as He did from Israel when He pointed them toward their inheritance.[6]

How can the searching, revealing nature of God's Word assist a diligent believer more fully to enjoy God's rest?

FAITH ALIVE

How can reliance on the Word of God make your life more restful and peaceful?

How can reliance on the Spirit of God make your life more restful and peaceful?

What things in your life tend to disrupt the rest and peace God wants you to enjoy in Christ Jesus? How should you deal with them?

1. "Moses," *Nelson's Illustrated Bible Dictionary* (Nashville: Thomas Nelson Publishers, 1986), 727–730.

2. "Wanderings of Israel," Ibid., 1091.

3. *Spirit-Filled Life Bible* (Nashville: Thomas Nelson Publishers, 1991), 1875, note on Hebrews 3:7–11.

4. Ibid., 1891, "Truth-in-Action through Hebrews."

5. Ibid., 1875, note on Hebrews 4:1.

6. Ibid., 1876, "Kingdom Dynamics: Hebrews 4:11–13, Understanding *Rhema* and *Logos*."

Lesson 4/The Best Help During Tempta-tion (4:14—5:11)

The day Fran showed up at an Indianapolis rescue mission asking for a room, he didn't look like a leader or a counselor. He had a change of underwear in his gym bag and a history of alcohol and drug abuse. He also had a newfound relationship with Jesus Christ that had not affected his drinking.

Fran had set out thirty years before to be a high school teacher and made it into his senior year of college. With only student teaching to go, his alcoholism cost him his career goal. In the Air Force, he parlayed recreational drug use into a profitable enterprise and a less than honorable discharge.

Drugs paid well with one hand, but with the other took away two marriages and the children from both. Finally he operated in both Phoenix and Indianapolis until the desire to settle down led to a third marriage and a legal job in Indianapolis. He began to think about God and the purpose of his life.

When Fran's third wife left him, despair set in. He stumbled across an evangelist on television and cried out to God like a drowning man clutching for a lifeline. He swung wildly between drunkenness and sobriety until the evening he checked into Wheeler Mission.

At the mission Fran discovered how to depend on the Lord Jesus for strength to deal with each day of life without escaping into a bottle. Three years later he became a chaplain at Wheeler Mission and emerged as a counselor uniquely equipped to understand the temptations and failures of the men he talked with every day.

A SYMPATHETIC FELLOW SUFFERER

The writer of Hebrews went to great pains in the first four chapters of his epistle to establish that the glorious, divine Son of God became a perfect but fully human man so that He could provide both salvation and the resources to live for Him. In the final three verses of chapter 4, the writer returned to the theme of the priesthood of Jesus last mentioned in 2:17 and 18. If Fran is equipped to sympathize with men addicted to alcohol and drugs, Jesus is equipped to sympathize with all human weakness.

What truth did the writer review when he referred to Jesus as "a great High Priest"? (Heb. 4:14; see 2:17)

What truth did the writer anticipate when he wrote that Jesus "has passed through the heavens"? (Heb. 4:14; see 9:23–28)

Christ Rose

Hebrews 4:14 concludes that Christians who recognize who Jesus is and what He has done will persevere in their confession of faith in Him. What do verses 15 and 16 imply about the ease or difficulty of maintaining a public confession of faith in Christ?

we will be Tempted

From Hebrews 4:15, what do you conclude about the nature of the temptations Jesus experienced on earth?

common of them all of them

WORD WEALTH

The Greek word translated "to tempt" is a neutral term that can mean both "to test" in the way God proves the strength of our faith (James 1:3) and "to tempt" in the way Satan appeals to us to sin (James 1:13). A particular difficult circumstance is neutral. God desires to use it to prove the strength of character His Spirit has produced in us. Satan desires to use it to lure us to respond sinfully in obedience to the flesh. God views the incident as a trial; Satan intends the same incident as a temptation.

What practical application did the writer of Hebrews draw from Jesus' experience of temptation? (Heb. 4:16)

he will understand us

The expression "throne of grace" occurs nowhere else in the New Testament. What do you think the writer of Hebrews wanted to say about God by calling the seat of His sovereignty "the throne of grace"? (Heb. 4:16)

that we mighty but worthy he is

WORD WEALTH

The word translated "boldly" (Heb. 4:16) has a lengthy classical Greek background connected to the democratic assemblies of the ancient city states. First, boldness assumed the right of a citizen to say anything. Second, it imposed a responsibility to speak truthfully. Finally, boldness implied the courage to speak in the presence of opponents.

The boldness encouraged in Hebrews 4:16 belongs to a citizen of the kingdom of heaven. Because of the intercession of Christ, a believer can speak his mind fully and frankly to God the Father. He must speak truthfully, and he or she need never fear an enemy at the throne of grace.

How does each of these divine qualities help us in different phases of our experience with temptation? (Heb. 4:16)

Mercy

Grace

BEHIND THE SCENES

Key Lessons in Faith (Heb. 4:16).[1] Faith accepts the fact that Jesus Christ died and was raised from the dead for our sins and has become our great High Priest.

Be bold in coming into the throne of God through the blood of Jesus Christ in prayer. Like little children running into the arms of their father, so we can come **boldly** into the presence of God through the blood of Jesus Christ and find help in the time of need.

Understand that although God is holy and righteous **we may obtain mercy** because Jesus Christ is our High Priest. In practical terms this means that we can come to God with our sins, failures, fears, and shortcomings and expect Him to cleanse us and restore us.

Finally, because Jesus Christ is our great High Priest we can expect to **find grace to help in time of need.** This means that God's unmerited favor is ours whenever we have needs or are in trouble. If God helped us and sent His power in our lives only when we deserved it, we would be in big trouble! However, because of Jesus Christ, God sends us His power and help even when we don't deserve it!

     ## FAITH ALIVE

How could meditating on the temptations Jesus suffered help you to understand the specific temptations you struggle with?

What temptation do you face that you wonder how Jesus Christ could fully understand?

Why is it harder for you to imagine His fully understanding *this* temptation?

What has God promised for even the most challenging of temptations?

A COMPASSIONATE INTERCESSOR

The writer of Hebrews seems to have been concerned that his description of Jesus as a merciful high priest would not fit with his readers' conceptions of a priest. He surveyed the general characteristics required of a high priest to show that Jesus' compassion was perhaps the most critical high priestly characteristic.

According to Hebrews 5:1–4, what is expected of a human high priest in each of these areas?

Dealing with sin

Dealing with sinners

Dealing with his own needs

Dealing with priestly honor

 BEHIND THE SCENES

The **high priest** was the supreme civil head of his people. Aaron held this position above his sons that was to continue in the firstborn of successive holders of the office. The high priest was distinguished from his fellow priests by the clothes he wore, the duties he performed, and the particular requirements placed upon him as the spiritual head of God's people.

Although the office of high priest was hereditary, its holder had to be without physical defect as well as holy in conduct (Lev. 21:6–8). A high priest was consecrated (installed in office) by an elaborate seven-day service at the tabernacle or temple (Exodus 29; Leviticus 8). He was cleansed by bathing, then dressed in the garments and symbols he must wear in his ministry and anointed with special oil. Sacrifices of sin offerings, burnt offerings, and consecration offerings were made for him; and he was anointed again with oil and blood of the sacrifice. Thus "sanctified" to serve as a priest and "consecrated" to offer sacrifice (Ex. 28:41; 29:9), he became "the saint [holy one] of the Lord" (Ps. 106:16).

The most important responsibility of the high priest was to conduct the service on the Day of Atonement, the tenth day of the seventh month each year. On this day he alone entered the Holy Place inside the veil before God. Having made sacrifice for himself and for the people, he brought the blood into the Most Holy Place and sprinkled it on the mercy seat, "God's throne." It is with this particular service that the ministry of Jesus as high priest is compared (Heb. 9:11–28).

WORD WEALTH

To have compassion in Hebrews 5:2 is a verb that occurs nowhere else in the Bible. It means to control one's emotions because of extenuating circumstances, in this case, the ignorance and wandering that human high priests share with the people. This moderate word is in contrast with the strong sympathy attributed to Jesus in 4:15.

Which of these high priestly characteristics apply fully to Jesus and how do they apply? (Heb. 5:1–4)

Which of these high priestly characteristics do not apply fully to Jesus and why not? (Heb. 5:1–4)

Why do you think it's important that God select His own High Priest? (Heb. 5:4)

 BIBLE EXTRA

Aaron was the first high priest of Israel in the Old Testament. Look up the following passages and record what you discover about him and his high priesthood.

Exodus 4:10–17

Exodus 7:1–7

Exodus 28:1, 2

Exodus 32: 1–6, 19–26

Leviticus 9:22

Numbers 6:23–27

Numbers 20:23–29

FAITH ALIVE

What would be frustrating and defeating about being represented before God by someone who had no idea about human weaknesses and frailties?

What are the implications of this passage for your pastor? How should he regard his frailties? How should you regard his frailties?

AN OBEDIENT SAVIOR

Fran is an effective counselor in a rescue mission because his knowledge and insights have been "perfected" by suffering. In his case the heavenly Father has redeemed the pain that resulted from sin and turned it into compassionate insight and firm direction. Jesus, however, is an insightful, suffering Savior because He experienced the strong pull of temptation, but He never gave in to the appeals of the Wicked One.

What evidence did the writer of Hebrews give that Jesus was appointed by God to be High Priest? (Heb. 5:5, 6)

What role in addition to priest did Melchizedek hold? (Heb. 5:6; see Gen. 14:18)

Does the quotation from Psalm 2:7 in Hebrews 5:5 relate more to the priestly role or the other role Jesus shares with Melchizedek? Why?

When did Jesus cry out in prayer for the Father to deliver Him from death? (Heb. 5:7; see Luke 22:39–46)

Does the wording of Hebrews 5:7 lead you to think the writer had in mind one instance of intense praying or more than one? What makes you think so?

What do you think Jesus dreaded with a "godly fear" as He anticipated dying for the sins of mankind? (Heb. 5:7; see Mark 14:33, 34; Luke 22:44; Matt. 27:46)

     ## WORD WEALTH

Learned obedience, in Hebrews 5:8, has the notion of "practiced obedience." Jesus did not learn obedience in the sense that He did not initially understand the concept or agree with it. He learned obedience in the sense that a baseball team infield learns to execute double plays. After the players are completely familiar with the concepts and skills, they practice them over and over. They become artists of double-play making. Jesus practiced obedience to the will of the Father until He became an artist of obedience.

In what sense and toward what end was Jesus "perfected," or brought to completion, by what He suffered? (Heb. 5:8, 9)

     ## WORD WEALTH

Jesus is called "the author of eternal salvation" in Hebrews 5:9. In Hebrews 2:10, by way of comparison, He was called "the captain of their salvation." "Captain" implied supremacy, source, and participant. Participation was important in the context of Hebrews 2 which stressed the fellowship of Jesus and His brothers.

"Author" signifies that Jesus is the personal cause of our salvation. He is not the cause in the sense of a catalyst that is separate from the resulting salvation. Jesus is the inseparable basis and grounds of eternal salvation.

Why did the writer of Hebrews use "obey" as a synonym for faith in Hebrews 5:9? What shade of meaning is added to the concept of faith by this word choice?

When you read Hebrews 5:10, 11, in which the writer dangles hints that he has more to say about Jesus and about his readers, what do these phrases make you anticipate?

"High Priest according to the order of Melchizedek"

"you have become dull of hearing"

 FAITH ALIVE

What spiritual burden have you cared enough about to offer to God in prayers and supplications with tears?

Read 2 Corinthians 10:3–5. What ideas ("arguments") or attitudes (things exalted "against the knowledge of God") related to this burden do you need to "cast down" by God's power in order to experience His victory in this matter (see Jesus' own struggle, Matt. 26:36–42)?

Compare Romans 12:1, 2 and Hebrews 13:9–15. What sacrifices may we offer to God as a way of identifying with Jesus' sacrifice? How will our offering these sacrifices help us experience God's power through our burdens?

What divine resource aids us beyond our own understanding as we pray in our "spiritual language"? (Rom. 8:26)

What spiritual discipline do you need to "learn" by disciplined repetition until it is second nature for you?

1. *Spirit-Filled Life Bible* (Nashville: Thomas Nelson Publishers, 1991), 1891, "Truth-in-Action through Hebrews."
2. "Priest, High," *Nelson's Illustrated Bible Dictionary* (Nashville: Thomas Nelson Publishers, 1986), 869–870.

Lesson 5/The Best Cure for Immaturity
(5:12—6:20)

He was in the sixth grade now—the last year of elementary school, and a new school at that. During recess on the playground on a sunny fall day, Peter punched him in the stomach during a general scuffle. It was an accident, but his abdomen stiffened after expelling his breath. Doubled over, he couldn't inhale. He couldn't even gasp.

He just made stupid grunts and started to cry. Peter was apologizing, but he could only see Peter's shoes from his doubled-over stance. Other shoes crowded around. And there among all those shoes while he couldn't breathe he realized something. Nobody else cried any more. He was the only one.

In fact he couldn't remember when any of his friends had last cried just because of a little hurt. Worse, he knew that crying was a way he got sympathy because he was small.

He knew all these things in the split-second before his solar plexus let him gulp some air. It hurt. But it felt good because he didn't cry.

"I'm all right," he croaked at Peter.

Growing up may hurt your stomach, but failure to grow up breaks hearts.

ADMIT YOUR SPIRITUAL AGE

On the anonymous Sunday school survey, one lady indicated her age as 65+. The only problem for the age-conscious woman was that the set of forms alternated male-female through the stack, and her husband had innocently written 74. By concealing her age she drew attention to herself.

From the information provided in Hebrews 5:12–14, describe the spiritual status of Hebrew Christians.

As it should have been

As it was

What did the writer of Hebrews mean to convey by the metaphor of needing milk rather than solid food? (Heb. 5:12, 13)

WORD WEALTH

"The first principles of the oracles of God" (Heb. 5:12) indicates the most basic ideas of the revealed Word of God. The Greeks had a word that meant the ABC's of something, and the writer of Hebrews used it here. The Hebrew Christians should have been teachers, but they were still working on the spiritual alphabet.

In Hebrews 6:1, in a related idea, the author challenged the immaturity of their relationship with Christ. In 5:12 his concern was their grasp of the Scripture. Because they were Hebrew Christians, these believers probably knew the biblical facts, but they were children in applying them to the tough issues of life.

How does a Christian reach the mature state when one can handle solid food? (Heb. 5:14)

Do you think the Hebrew Christians realized that they were immature for their spiritual age? Why did you reach that conclusion?

 FAITH ALIVE

What happens to the personal lives of Christians who insist they are spiritually mature when, in fact, they are still children? *When the wind comes you can keep study*

What happens to immature Christians and their church when they assume leadership or teaching roles? (see James 3)

What might it take from God to convince an immature Christian that it is past time to start growing up spiritually?

How does one move from immaturity to maturity in Jesus Christ?

STAY AWAY FROM THE EDGE

Take a group of people to the edge of a cliff, and you get a number of reactions. Some won't go near the edge. Nothing can get them near it. Others lie down and peer cautiously over. A brave group steps to the edge and stands there. A very few feel an urge—a strange, strong compulsion—to jump.

In what way is each of these doctrinal topics in Hebrews 6:1, 2 foundational to a maturing Christian life?

Repentance from dead works

Faith toward God

The doctrine of baptisms

Laying on of hands (see Acts 8:17–19; 1 Tim. 4:14)

Resurrection of the dead

Eternal judgment

WORD WEALTH

The discussion of the elementary principles of Christ translates another unusual Greek construction in Hebrews. "Discussion" translates *logos.* "Elementary principles" translates *arche,* the word for "beginning" in John 1:1. "Christ" is actually *"the* Christ," the Messiah. The writer urged these Hebrew Christians to get past discussing and expounding the kindergarten concepts about Jesus the Messiah.

To what extent did the progress of the Hebrew Christians from lingering immaturity to long-overdue maturity depend on each of these factors?

Their choice (Heb. 6:1)

The activity of God (Heb. 6:3)

The writer of Hebrews issues a severe warning to people who have had certain spiritual experiences in the past. What would you ordinarily assume these expressions mean? (Heb. 6:4)

Enlightened

Tasted the heavenly gift

Partakers of the Holy Spirit

Tasted the good Word of God

Tasted . . . the powers of the age to come

What did the writer of Hebrews hypothesize to be impossible for those who had these past spiritual experiences? (Heb. 6:4–6)

 ## BEHIND THE SCENES

The important practical issue in v. 6 is the meaning of "fall away." Can a believer fall away without knowing it in the course of backsliding, or must a believer decide to reject Christ even as he or she once chose to receive Him?

"The language of vv. 4 and 5 clearly describes those who have experienced the saving grace of God, and the language of v. 6 denotes a complete disowning of Christ, a deliberate and decisive abandonment of the Christian faith. The people described are not backsliders but apostates. They have not merely fallen into sin but have denounced Christ."[1]

Notice that Hebrews 6:4–6 begins with "for," which introduces the **reason** the writer is "not laying again the foundation" but instead urging his readers "on to perfection" (v. 1). That is, the whole discussion about those who fall away and therefore cannot be renewed again to repentance (v. 6) serves mainly to **explain** and **motivate.** These verses explain why the writer

- will not lay the foundation again (because it would be of no benefit to those who have fallen away), but instead
- urges his readers "on to perfection" (because, while they are immature [5:12], the way they become mature is precisely by going on, not by again laying the foundation).

These verses also motivate the Hebrew Christians
- **away from** the example of the apostates who, under pressure from non-Christian Jews, have renounced Christ and thus forfeited inheriting what God has promised; and
- **toward** the example of "those who through faith and patience inherit the promises" (v. 12).

A brief paraphrase may help clarify the aim of Hebrews 5:12—6:12:

> True enough, you are immature as believers when I would expect you to be much more mature. But there's no point in my spending more time laying the foundation of your faith all over again; it's time for you to be up and growing unto maturity! Laying the foundation again would not help you one bit, nor would it help those who fully experienced salvation but then consciously, deliberately, and repeatedly disowned Christ and remain in that state to this day. Nothing can help them!
> And while you should be sobered by their state, the very fact that I am writing to help you shows my confidence that you (unlike them) will follow the example of the faithful and thus inherit all God's promises. Let's go on!

Hebrews acknowledges what each of us knows is true—genuine believers do sin (Heb. 12:1), but without falling away. The act of falling away is not a matter of how often or of how many different ways one sins. "Falling away" in Hebrews refers to apostasy—the full, continuous denial of Christ as Lord and

Savior by those who once trusted in and obeyed Him. How can any be saved who persist in denying the only Savior?

BEHIND THE SCENES

If I sin, will I lose my salvation? (Heb. 6:4–6)

Can you conceive of somebody adopting a child and then throwing her out on the street because she falls while learning to walk? When we are saved, we are adopted into the family of God. We must, out of love on one hand and godly fear on the other, seek to live a life that is pleasing to Him. But the idea that one act of sin would cause someone to be thrown out of God's family is not in the Bible (1 John 1:7, 9). However, acts of sin or rebellion will take away the joy of your salvation.

If one continues in a course of known sin, assurance of one's salvation may be lost, but that is not the same as an actual loss of one's salvation. A person born of the Spirit of God will be drawn back to repentance every time he sins.

Beyond that, we do read in Hebrews 10:29 that if somebody actually says the blood of Jesus Christ is a common (unholy) thing and renounces the salvation he has received, then that person may have lost it all. But the same book says, "But, beloved, we are confident of better things concerning you" (Heb. 6:9).[2]

FOLLOW THE LEADERS

Adam needed Eve. Moses needed Aaron. David needed Jonathan. Even Nehemiah confided in his diary. Jesus sent the disciples out by two's, and the apostles followed that example. Almighty God fellowships within the Trinity, and He expects Christians to live out the reality of their salvation within the context of the church, the body of Christ.

The writer of Hebrews did not address his readers often with a title. When he did, what was it usually? (Heb. 3:1, 12; 10:19; 13:22)

What did he call them in Hebrews 6:9?

Why do you think he used a term of endearment at this point?

How did the writer of Hebrews base his confidence concerning his readers on these two foundations? (Heb. 6:9, 10)

The character of God

"Things that accompany salvation"

What was the writer's desire for his readers? (Heb. 6:11, 12)

WORD WEALTH

To imitate carries a connotation of laziness and lack of originality to the modern mind. In the New Testament, this word approximates the contemporary concepts of following a model or learning from a mentor. It was one of Paul's favorite expressions for learning from others (1 Cor. 4:16; 11:1; Eph. 5:1; Phil. 3:17; 1 Thess. 1:6; 2:14).

What role do you think each of these spiritual virtues plays in the writer's desire for his readers? (Heb. 6:11, 12)

Hope

Faith

Patience

For Hebrew Christians of the first century, who would they have looked to in the past as diligent inheritors of the promises in order to imitate them?

WORD WEALTH

Hope is a difficult biblical word because we associate wishfulness and indefiniteness with it. "Hope" in the Bible refers to something real but unseen. The realities of the spiritual world—such as God, angels, heaven, love, righteousness, peace, salvation, etc.—are foundational to the realities of the physical world. A biblical "hope" is more certain than the ground on which you stand. And "the blessed hope," therefore, is the spiritual reality and certainty of the Return of Christ. One of the things faith does is comprehend and trust the "hopes."

 ## FAITH ALIVE

What Christians from the past do you admire and how can their examples help you live hopefully, faithfully, and patiently?

What Christians should you imitate now? How do they exhibit hope, faith, and patience?

DON'T DOUBT GOD

The old Indian was a savant. No one knew how he did it—least of all himself. The contractor kept Norman on the payroll to tell him how many cubic feet were in an air conditioning system in a skyscraper under construction. The new engineers never believed Norman when he surveyed the drawings, looked at the superstructure, and announced his figures. In those days they got out slide rules and worked feverishly for some time before admitting Norman was close enough for practical purposes. The regular crew had long since stopped doubting Norman.

Noman's insight was an intellectual quirk. The wisdom and omniscience of God is a fundamental fact of reality. The plans and promises of God are altogether trustworthy. No one should doubt them for a moment.

What happened when Abraham, the great biblical example of faith, diligently pursued the promise of God? (Heb. 6:13–15)

What importance can be attached to the fact that God swore an oath, and an oath by Himself at that, to fulfill His promise to Abraham? (Heb. 6:13, 16)

 BEHIND THE SCENES

The concept of **promise** is vital to understanding the continuity of God's saving work through the Old Testament into the New Testament. The promise of a blessing made by God to Abraham and his descendants is the fundamental promise that all other biblical promises and covenants explain and expand (Gen. 12:2, 3; Rom. 9:6–8; Gal. 3:15–18; 4:28).

When the writer of Hebrews began to deal with persevering to the end and receiving the reward of a lifetime of mature discipleship, he naturally used the covenant phrase "inherit the promises" (Heb. 6:12) and started using Abraham as the ultimate example of faith. From here to the end of Hebrews, "promises" or "the promise" refer to the benefits, blessings, and goals of salvation in Christ as the fulfillment of the New Covenant (for example, 9:15, 10:36; and 11:39, 40).

What are the two immutable (unchanging) things that guarantee God's blessing on people? (Heb. 6:17, 18)

What recommendation did the writer of Hebrews make to his immature readers who may have been tempted by doubt or persecution to apostatize from their faith in Christ? (Heb. 6:18, 19)

 BEHIND THE SCENES

In Hebrews 6:19, 20 the writer introduces the tabernacle as a visualization of the heavenly realm where the presence of God is. Hebrews expands on this theme in chapter 9. In the final verses of chapter 6, the writer alludes to the high priest entering the Most Holy Place once a year on the Day of Atonement. By contrast, Jesus the eternal High Priest is permanently in the Presence.

Why should Jesus in the presence of God have served as an anchor for the souls of immature and doubting Hebrew Christians? (Heb. 6:19, 20)

FAITH ALIVE

What promises of God do you go back to repeatedly as reference points for faith when you feel doubt creeping into your soul?

What do you feel that you have in common spiritually with Abraham, Moses, David, and other Old Testament recipients of promises?

Write a prayer of praise to the Lord Jesus in which you tell Him what it means to you that He anchors your soul in the presence of God.

---

1. *Spirit-Filled Life Bible* (Nashville: Thomas Nelson Publishers, 1991), 1878, note on Hebrews 6:4–6.

2. Ibid., 1997, "Spiritual Answers to Hard Questions: If I sin, will I lose my salvation?"

Lesson 6/The Best Access to God (7:1–28)

In the opening pages of *War and Peace,* a faded Russian aristocratic lady desperately but determinedly pursues the appointment of her son Boris to an officer's commission in the army. She has no money. She has no influence. But she has access to certain powerful people—the remnants of the wealth and power that had once been hers. And she has a mother's tenacity.

First she badgers the prince into asking the Emperor for the commission for Boris. He doesn't want to use up a favor on the old woman, but he knows she won't give him peace unless he does. Then she assails Boris's godfather, the Count, to outfit her son in the best uniforms and kit. But, alas, the Count is dying and cannot help her.

As a reader, you feel like Anna Mikhaylovna Drubetskaya represented more, as though the whole Russian aristocracy might be fading before the upstart Frenchman Napoleon. Maybe the student Pierre is right and access to the Emperor and leading families doesn't matter. Perhaps it would be best to curry favor with the diplomats who can reach Napoleon.

That is just a story, and just the opening scenes at that. The Epistle to the Hebrews describes realities in the heavenly realm and sees clear to the end of things. One of the major issues is access to the presence of God.

BETTER PREDECESSOR THAN THE OLD WAY

Anna Mikhaylovna operated according to the principle that the best families dictated what was right. Pierre believed in the rights of man. Her approach made Princess Anna an aristocrat. His approach made Pierre a democrat. The writer of

Hebrews asserted to his readers that it would make all the difference in the world whether they approached God through the priestly descendants of Levi or the priestly Descendant of Melchizedek.

Melchizedek was mentioned without explanation in Hebrews 5:6, 10 and 6:20. In Hebrews 7:1 and the first part of verse 2, what historical information is provided about Melchizedek?

In Hebrews 7:2, 3 what interpretive conclusions did the writer of Hebrews draw from Melchizedek's titles and lack of background information?

 BEHIND THE SCENES

Melchizedek was a king of Salem (Jerusalem) and priest of the Most High God (Gen. 14:18–20; Ps. 110:4; Heb. 5:6–11; 6:20—7:28). Melchizedek's sudden appearance and disappearance in the Book of Genesis are somewhat mysterious. Melchizedek and Abraham first met after Abram's defeat of Chedorlaomer and his three allies. Melchizedek presented bread and wine to Abraham and his weary men, demonstrating friendship and religious kinship. He bestowed a blessing on Abraham in the name of El Elyon ("God Most High") and praised God for giving Abraham a victory in battle (Gen. 14:18–20).

Abraham presented Melchizedek with a tithe (a tenth) of all the booty he had gathered. By this act Abraham indicated that he recognized Melchizedek as a fellow-worshiper of the one true God as well as a priest who ranked higher spiritually than himself. Melchizedek's existence shows that there were people other than Abraham and his family who served the true God.

In Psalm 110, a messianic psalm written by David (Matt. 22:43), Melchizedek is seen as a type of Christ. This theme is repeated in the Book of Hebrews, where both Melchizedek and Christ are considered kings of righteousness and peace. By citing Melchizedek and his unique priesthood as a type, the writer shows that Christ's new priesthood is superior to the old Levitical order and the priesthood of Aaron (Heb. 7:1–10).

Attempts have been made to identify Melchizedek as an imaginary character named Shem, an angel, the Holy Spirit, Christ, and others. All are products of speculation, not historical fact; and it is impossible to reconcile them with the theological argument of Hebrews. Melchizedek was a real, historical king-priest who served as a type for the greater King-Priest who was to come, Jesus Christ.[1]

 BIBLE EXTRA

Read Genesis 14 in which verses 18–20 contain all that the Bible says about the mysterious Melchizedek. In the story of the battle of the kings, Melchizedek, king of Salem, stands in contrast to the king of Sodom. How did Abraham's response to Melchizedek contrast with his response to the king of Sodom?

Why do you think Abraham gave a tithe of the spoils to Melchizedek?

A thousand years after the time of Abraham and a thousand years before the Epistle to the Hebrews, David wrote Psalm 110 and made reference in verse 4 to the eternal priesthood of Melchizedek. Already David was fascinated with the absence of detail about this great priest's lineage and his potential prophetic symbolism about the Messiah. Considering how much the writer of Hebrews makes of Psalm 110:4, it's interesting that no other New Testament writer picked up on the prophetic connection between Melchizedek and the Messiah.

Why did Abraham give a tithe to Melchizedek? (Heb. 7:4; see Gen. 14:18–20)

Why did the descendants of Abraham pay tithes to Levi? (Heb. 7:5)

What kinds of evidence did the writer of Hebrews present for the superiority of Melchizedek to Levi? (Heb. 7:4–9)

BEHIND THE SCENES
_____

    Levi was the third son of Jacob and Leah (Gen. 29:34). He was not an admirable man. Along with Simeon he massacred the inhabitants of Shechem in revenge for the rape of their sister Dinah (34:25, 30). When Jacob blessed his sons before his death, he prophesied that Simeon and Levi would be scattered among the other tribes because of their cruel wrath (49:5–7). Levi died in Egypt at age 137 (Ex. 6:16).

In time Moses and Aaron descended from Levi (Ex. 2:1ff). A grandson of Aaron halted a plague by acting ruthlessly for righteousness (Num. 25:11–13). The Levites were scattered through Israel as priests in part because of Levi's cruelty and in part because of Phineas' devotion to holiness. It's instructive that God chose a tribe in desperate need of forgiveness to represent Himself to the rest of the people.

 FAITH ALIVE

It's hard to get very excited today about theological discussions about Melchizedek and Levi; that is, until you understand that Melchizedek is a type of Christ. He represents a new, liberating priesthood which invites you and me to come directly to our glorious High Priest, Jesus Christ, with any problem or burden (Heb. 7:20–22).

What should it mean in terms of how you relate to Jesus that the One who provides forgiveness of sins and access to God also has the following royal titles?

King of righteousness

King of peace

BETTER PROMISES THAN THE OLD WAY

In *War and Peace* the tired, aristocratic world of old Russia could promise wealth and comfort only to a few families of privilege. The vigorous, revolutionary world of Napoleon promised advancement to all people of ambition and courage. Unfortunately for the characters in the novel who claimed these promises, neither world could deliver on its promises. Fortunately for the readers of Hebrews, the Lord Jesus keeps His promises.

Since David predicted a new priesthood after the order of Melchizedek in Psalm 110:4, what did that imply about the Levitical priesthood and the Mosaic Law? (Heb. 7:11, 12)

What is different about the new priesthood of the Lord Jesus in comparison with the Levitical priesthood? (Heb. 7:13–15)

What is different about the new promise of the Lord Jesus in comparison with the law of Moses? (Heb. 7:16–19)

WORD WEALTH

The word translated **perfect** indicates the final stage toward which a process is moving. Often "maturity" is a more accurate translation when the word is applied to finite humans. Look up the following uses of this term in the first seven chapters of Hebrews and summarize why the old priesthood and law were inadequate for perfection. (2:10; 5:9; 6:1; 7:11, 19)

Compare Hebrews 7:19 with 6:19, 20. Why do you think the new promises are called "a better hope, through which we draw near to God"?

FAITH ALIVE

What would you find the most distressing aspect of trying to keep the Mosaic Law?

When you think about the difficulties of Christian discipleship, what encouragement do you find in reflecting that you have promises based on "the power of an endless life"?

BETTER PERSONNEL THAN THE OLD WAY

In *War and Peace* imperial Russia depended on an army commanded in large part by men agreeable to its bureaucracies. Napoleon fielded an army commanded by daring military minds akin to his own. Russia could rely on her winters more than her leaders. In the Book of Hebrews also, the new way has better leaders than the old way.

The seventh chapter of Hebrews has built to this conclusion. No priest has ever been a priest like Jesus Christ.

What qualities of the High Priesthood of Jesus were established by God's oath? (Heb. 7:20–22)

Why do you think the writer of Hebrews quoted Psalm 110:4 so many times? What effect is created for you by the repetition? (Heb. 5:6, 10; 7:17, 21)

What benefits accrue to people because of the eternality of the priesthood of Jesus? (Heb. 7:23–25)

WORD WEALTH

Unchangeable translates another of the many Greek words in Hebrews that appear nowhere else in the New Testament. The sense of the term seems to be that no one can harm or violate the character of whatever is in view, in this case the High Priesthood of Jesus Christ.

WORD WEALTH

To make intercession. To fall in with, meet with in order to converse. From this description of a casual encounter, the word progresses to the idea of pleading with a person on behalf of another, although at times the petition may be against another. In Romans 8:27 the Holy Spirit intercedes for the saints, and in verse 34 Christ is at the right hand of the Father interceding for believers. Both Spirit and Son continually engage the Father in conversation on our behalf.[2]

In what sense is it fitting, or in keeping with human needs, that Jesus be a High Priest with each of these characteristics? (Heb. 7:26)

Holy

Harmless (innocent)

Undefiled

Separate from sinners (set apart)

Become higher than the heavens

Why was the once-for-all sacrifice of Jesus superior to the repeated Levitical sacrifices? (Heb. 7:27)

Why was the oath-appointed High Priest better than the law-appointed high priests? (Heb. 7:28)

Why is it important that the Son "has been perfected forever"? (Heb. 7:28; see 2:10; 5:8, 9; 7:19)

How do you think we can find comfort and encouragement both in the thorough temptation Jesus endured (Heb. 2:18; 4:14–16) and in His complete holiness and moral detachment from sinfulness? (7:26)

 FAITH ALIVE

The Epistle to the Hebrews reveals just how carefully God constructed the Mosaic Law and Levitical order of worship to prepare the way for redemption in Christ. Everything in some way illustrated an aspect of the spiritual reality the Christ would make real. What has impressed you most so far about the use of the Old Testament by the writer of Hebrews?

What comfort do you find in knowing that the Son of God is continually interceding on your behalf with the Father? What has He been talking with God about for you?

What does Jesus know about your temptations that you don't know because He is the High Priest who never yielded to temptation?

1. "Melchizedek," *Nelson's Illustrated Bible Dictionary* (Nashville: Thomas Nelson Publishers, 1986), 694–695.

2. *Spirit-Filled Life Bible* (Nashville: Thomas Nelson Publishers, 1991), 1880, "Word Wealth: Hebrews 7:25, make intercession."

Lesson 7/The Best Promise Made by God
(8:1–13)

Pierre, the hero in *War and Peace*, could not find meaning in life. He had education, money, a beautiful wife, and social position, but he could not control his sensuality. No matter how much philanthropy he indulged in, no matter how many times he resolved to live morally, eventually Pierre gave in to drunken carousing and self-loathing.

One night in a train compartment on a journey, an ascetic old man introduced Pierre to the mysteries and ceremonies of a cult-like religious teaching. With all of his energy and moral resolution, Pierre devoted himself to this system, in what he thought was an attempt to help his fellow man and purify his soul. But it never quite worked. The ideals of this false religious teaching appeared noble at first, but Pierre inevitably fell frustratingly short of its impossible demands.

Years later in a French prisoner-of-war camp Pierre met a peasant named Karataev who was at peace, and he discovered that God is a Person who has a will for each life. The impersonal and false god to whom he had been introduced before was a demanding taskmaster who pointed out every deviation from perfection and never forgave or comforted. Pierre opened himself to the true God in Christ and was transformed from within by better promises based on the Bible and not man-made ideas.

In a sense, Pierre's story is the story of every person. We all live either by the principle of the law and our own man-made ideas of perfection or by God's principle of grace found in the New Testament. If we live by law then it's all up to us to please Him by our efforts. But if we live by grace we rely completely on God to make us pleasing to Him. The Book of

Hebrews reminds us that God once used a law to prepare mankind to respond enthusiastically to grace.

THE BEST PROMISE IS HEAVENLY

When Pierre was seduced by the teachings of this false religion, he thought they were spiritual and ennobling. Experience taught him that self-improvement was ultimately an earthly enterprise. He needed to escape the limitations of earthly systems and his own moral weakness.

Describe the scene of the High Priestly ministry of Jesus (Heb. 8:1, 2).

 BEHIND THE SCENES

Old Testament priests always stood when they ministered in the early tabernacle and the later temple (Heb. 10:11). There were no chairs among the furnishings of the Holy Place. The priestly work was never completed. It was always necessary for the priests to be available to offer still another sacrifice for sin.

Because Jesus offered one sacrifice at one point in time for all sins of all people in all times, He can sit down (Heb. 1:3; 8:1; 10:12). Because He perfectly fulfilled the plans of the Father and has been exalted above all others, Christ is seated at the right hand of God. Because He initiated a new and better way to God after making the ultimate revelation of Him to humans, Christ is magnified with all of the majesty associated with the throne of God (Heb. 8:1; compare Ezek. 1:22, 26; Rev. 4:2, 5, 6).

How does this High Priestly ministry relate to the physical absence of Jesus from the earth during the present age? (see Eph. 1:20; Col. 3:1)

WORD WEALTH

Minister is a compound word made from *laos,* "people," and *ergon,* "work"; hence, working for the people. The word first denoted someone who rendered public service at his own expense, then generally signified a public servant, a minister. In the New Testament it is used of earthly rulers (Rom. 13:6); the apostle Paul (Rom. 15:16); Epaphroditus, who attended to Paul's needs (Phil. 2:25); angels (Heb. 1:7); and Christ (Heb. 8:2).[1]

How can the Lord Jesus serve people from His heavenly tabernacle? (Heb. 8:2)

 ### WORD WEALTH

Sanctuary and **tabernacle** both refer to the heavenly presence of God. **Sanctuary** translates the plural neuter adjective "holies," which is a shortened form of "holy of holies" (Most Holy Place, NKJV), the inner room of the tabernacle where the ark of the covenant was kept. **Tabernacle** translates the common word for "tent." God is a nomad whose presence is wherever He wants it to be. The fact that Jesus is in the heavens does not separate Him from people as much as one might think.

How did the writer of Hebrews conclude that Jesus could not have been an earthly priest? (Heb. 8:3–5)

Although the writer didn't come right out and say so, how do you know from what he did say that the offering made by Jesus was better than those offered by earthly priests? (Heb. 8:3, 5)

BIBLE EXTRA

In Hebrews 8:8, the writer quoted Exodus 25:40 as evidence that God gave Moses exact directions for constructing the tabernacle and its furnishings. Read Exodus 25—27 for the complete tabernacle pattern the Lord revealed to Moses on Mount Sinai. Compare the instructions with the illustrations below.

THE PLAN OF THE TABERNACLE[2]

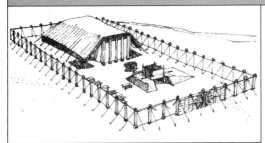

The tabernacle was to provide a place where God might dwell among His people. The term *tabernacle* sometimes refers to the tent, including the holy place and the Most Holy, which was covered with embroidered curtains. But in other places it refers to the entire complex, including the curtained court in which the tent stood.

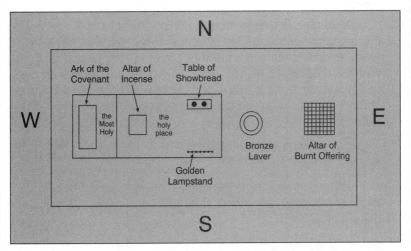

This illustration shows the relative positions of the tabernacle furniture used in Israelite worship. The tabernacle is enlarged for clarity. See also Chart: The Furniture of the Tabernacle, p. 92.

Hebrews 8:6 summarizes three ideas the writer has emphasized earlier in the book. What has the writer of Hebrews already said about each of these subjects?

"He has obtained a more excellent ministry" (see Heb. 2:14–18; 7:23–28)

"He is also Mediator of a better covenant" (see Heb. 7:12–22)

"Which was established on better promises" (see Heb. 6:13–20)

 WORD WEALTH

Mediator is a legal term denoting the role of Christ as the arbitrator between God and humanity. Hebrews goes to great lengths to demonstrate that Christ is fully God (1:2, 3) and fully human (2:14–18). In His person Christ brings God and humanity together. By means of His sacrifice for sins he reconciles sinful mankind to holy God.

 FAITH ALIVE

What do you think is the most frustrating aspect of trying to please God by keeping all sorts of legalistic rules as some people try to do?

To you what is the most liberating aspect of the priestly ministry of Jesus Christ that frees you from bondage to the Law?

What confidence does it give you to know that you have a Mediator in heaven at the right hand of God?

THE BEST PROMISE IS GRACIOUS

In *War and Peace* Pierre found the law of a false religious system to be rigid and impossible to keep. When he discovered the gracious love and forgiveness of God amid the squalor and terrors of the prisoner-of-war camp, his heart was changed. The first thing people noticed about Pierre after his release from captivity was that he was at peace for the first time in his life.

What was wrong with the Old Covenant that made a new one necessary? (Heb. 8:7–12)

 WORD WEALTH

Finding fault translates a verb that means "to blame." In Hebrews 8:8, the writer says "finding fault with *them.*" The Law is holy, just, and good (Rom. 7:12), but the weakness of human flesh renders the Law ineffective in leading *people* to righteousness (Rom. 8:3, 4). The criticism of Jeremiah is ultimately aimed at the sinfulness of the Israelites who could not keep the covenant they made with God. In His mercy and grace, God made provision for a New Covenant that addressed the weakness of the flesh.

What are the main characteristics of the New Covenant? (Heb. 8:10–12)

Contrast the Old and New Covenants in each of these categories. (Heb. 8:7–13)

	OLD COVENANT	NEW COVENANT
When made		
With whom		
Benefits		
Evaluation		

From what is said to be superior about the New Covenant, what can be assumed were deficiencies in the Old? (Heb. 8:10–12)

BIBLE EXTRA

The two major passages in the Old Testament about the New Covenant are Jeremiah 31:31–34 (the one quoted in Hebrews 8) and Ezekiel 36:25–27. Read these prophetic passages in their contexts and summarize the main provisions of the covenant.

BEHIND THE SCENES

The prophet Jeremiah ministered to the southern kingdom of Judah before, during, and after the final Babylonian conquest of Jerusalem. He witnessed the results of long-term, habitual covenant breaking on the part of the people of God. Perhaps the most wonderful revelation granted Jeremiah by the Lord was the promise of a New Covenant that would be radically different from the old one. This New Covenant would be written on the hearts of God's people rather than on tablets of stone (Jer. 31:33). Anyone who breaks this covenant must violate the new nature given him or her by God Himself.

Jeremiah's vision was messianic. It looked forward to the end times when both Israel and Judah would be gathered from their dispersions and enjoying peace and prosperity (Jer. 30:1—31:30). It assumed a new spiritual dynamic capable of totally renewing human hearts (31:33). The Epistle to the Hebrews provides the rest of the story.

BEHIND THE SCENES

Jesus' ministry is performed under the covenant of God's grace, wrought within the mind and hearts of believers by the power of the Holy Spirit. Thus, God established a personal covenant relationship with His people, based not on a compelling force from without, but on an impelling power from within.[3]

According to the writer of Hebrews, what is the effect of the establishment of the New Covenant on the old one? (Heb. 8:13)

In what way has the New Covenant replaced the Old?

 FAITH ALIVE

How have you sensed in your Christian experience that the Spirit of God has written on your heart some part of the truth of God that changes you?

What do you find most comforting and encouraging about the grace of God expressed in the New Covenant?

1. *Spirit-Filled Life Bible* (Nashville: Thomas Nelson Publishers, 1991), 1872, 1873, "Word Wealth: Hebrews 1:7, ministers."
2. Ibid., 120, Illustration: "The Plan of the Tabernacle."
3. Ibid., 1880, note on Hebrews 8:8–10.

Lesson 8/The Best Purification (9:1–28)

Lady Macbeth urged her husband to murder Duncan, King of Scotland, so that he could be king in Duncan's place. In the scenes of the play after the murder, references to blood represent guilt and references to sleep represent innocence. In terror Macbeth told his wife, "Methought I heard a voice cry, 'Sleep no more! / Macbeth doth murder sleep'—the innocent sleep."[1]

Lady Macbeth scoffed at her husband's fears. "Go get some water / And wash this filthy witness from your hand," she ordered.[2]

"Will all great Neptune's ocean wash this blood / Clean from my hand?" Macbeth wondered. "No, this my hand will rather / The multitudinous seas incarnadine, / Making the green one red."[3]

Lady Macbeth was furious at her husband's cowardice in the face of his monstrous crime. She thought she was beyond the reach of conscience, but soon she discovered she could not sleep peacefully. In her troubled slumber she paced Dunsinane castle rubbing her hands together trying vainly to wash the blood from them and from her soul. "Out, damned spot! Out I say! One, two—why, then 'tis time to do't! Hell is murky," she muttered.[4]

The Bible attaches tremendous significance to the shedding of blood. Murderous bloodshed defiles the land in a way unparalleled by other sins (Gen. 4:10, 11; 9:5, 6; Num. 35:3, 34). By the same token, sacrificial bloodshed has purifying capability (Lev. 16:11–19; 17:11; Heb. 9:14, 22). It was inevitable that the writer of Hebrews would come to this point: the blood of Christ provides a better purification from sins than the blood of sacrificial animals.

SYMBOLIC PURIFICATION

The writer of Hebrews has already reasoned that the earthly tabernacle which Israel built in the wilderness at Mount Sinai symbolized heavenly realities about the presence of God. It follows logically that the sacrifices of the tabernacle also symbolized heavenly realities about atonement for sins.

AT A GLANCE

THE FURNITURE OF THE TABERNACLE⁵

Ark of the Covenant
(Ex. 25:10–22)
The ark was most sacred of all the furniture in the tabernacle. Here the Hebrews kept a copy of the Ten Commandments, which summarized the whole covenant.

Bronze Laver
(Ex. 30:17–21)
It was to the laver of bronze that the priests would come for cleansing. They must be pure to enter the presence of God.

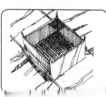

Altar of Burnt Offering
(Ex. 27:1–8)
Animal sacrifices were offered on this altar, located in the court in front of the tabernacle. The blood of the sacrifice was sprinkled on the four horns of the altar.

Gold Lampstand
(Ex. 25:31–40)
The gold lampstand stood in the holy place, opposite the table of showbread. It held seven lamps, flat bowls in which a wick lay with one end in the oil of the bowl and the lighted end hanging out.

Table of Showbread
(Ex. 25:23–30)
The table of showbread was a stand on which the offerings were placed. Always in God's presence on the table were the 12 loaves of bread representing the 12 tribes.

Altar of Incense
(Ex. 30:1–10)
The altar of incense inside the tabernacle was much smaller than the altar of burnt offering outside. The incense burned on the altar was a perfume of a sweet-smelling aroma.

The first covenant focused on the system of sacrifices and festivals centered around the tabernacle. Refer to the illustrations of the tabernacle and its furnishings in lesson 7 and directly above. Describe the furnishings of the first room of the tabernacle. (Heb. 9:2)

Describe the furnishings in or associated with the "Holiest of All" behind the veil. (Heb. 9:3–5)

 BEHIND THE SCENES

Cherubim are winged angelic beings, often associated with worship and praise of God. The cherubim are first mentioned in the Bible in Genesis 3:24. When God drove Adam and Eve from the Garden of Eden, He placed cherubim at the east end of the garden, "and a flaming sword which turned every way, to guard the way to the tree of life."

According to the prophets, cherubim belong to the category of unfallen angels; at one time, however, Satan, or Lucifer, was a cherub (Ezek. 28:14, 16), until he rebelled against God (Is. 14:12–14; Ezek. 28:12–19).

Symbolic representations of the cherubim were used in the tabernacle in the wilderness. Two cherubim made of gold were stationed at the two ends of the mercy seat, above the ark of the covenant in the Most Holy Place, or Holiest of All (Ex. 25:17–22; 1 Chr. 28:18; Heb. 9:5). Artistic designs of cherubim decorated the ten curtains (Ex. 26:1; 36:8) and the veil (Ex. 28:31; 2 Chr. 3:14) of the tabernacle.

When Solomon built the temple, he ordered that two cherubim be made of olive wood and overlaid with gold. Each measured ten cubits (4.6 meters or 15 feet) (1 Kin. 6:23–28; 8:6, 7; 2 Chr. 3:10–13; 5:7, 8). These gigantic cherubim were placed inside the inner sanctuary, or in the Most Holy Place in the temple. Their wings were spread over the ark of the covenant. The woodwork throughout the temple was decorated with engraved figures of cherubim, trees, and flowers (1 Kin. 6:28–35; 7:29, 36; 2 Chr. 3:7).[6]

The mention of the golden pot with manna and Aaron's rod that budded relates the tabernacle description by the writer of Hebrews to the time of the wilderness wandering (Ex. 16:33; Num. 17:1–10). Why do you think the writer took his readers back to the days when the tabernacle and its offerings were brand new?

Why do you think the writer of Hebrews associated gold so many times with the Holiest of All? (Heb. 9:4)

WORD WEALTH

Mercy seat translates a Greek word found in the New Testament only here and in Romans 3:25. The word is quite common in the Septuagint, the Greek Old Testament, where it primarily denotes the mercy seat, the lid of gold above the ark of the covenant. In this verse it has that meaning, indicating the place of atonement. The root meaning of this Greek word (*hilasterion*) is that of appeasing and placating an offended god. Applied to the sacrifice of Christ in that regard, the word suggests that Christ's death was propitiatory, averting the wrath of God from the sinner.[7]

Under the old covenant with its earthly tabernacle, who could approach God and how free was their access? (Heb. 9:6, 7)

 BEHIND THE SCENES

The tenth day of the seventh month of the Hebrew calendar was set aside as the Day of Atonement, a day of public fasting and humiliation. On this day the nation of Israel sought atonement for its sins (Lev. 23:27; 16:29; Num. 29:7). This day fell in the month equivalent to our August, and it was preceded by special Sabbaths (Lev. 23:24). The only fasting period required by the Law (Lev. 16:29; 23:31), the Day of Atonement was a recognition of man's inability to make an atonement for his sins. It was a solemn, holy day accompanied by elaborate ritual (Lev. 16; Heb. 10:1–10).

The high priest who officiated on this day first sanctified himself by taking a ceremonial bath and putting on white garments (Lev. 16:4). Then he had to make atonement for himself and other priests by sacrificing a bullock (Num. 29:8). God dwelt on the mercy seat in the temple, but no person could approach it except through the mediation of the high priest, who offered the blood of sacrifice.

After sacrificing a bullock, the high priest chose a goat for a sin-offering and sacrificed it. Then he sprinkled its blood on and above the mercy seat (Lev. 16:12, 14, 15). Finally the scapegoat bearing the sins of the people was sent into the wilderness (Lev. 16:20–22). This scapegoat symbolized the pardon for sin brought through the sacrifice (Gal. 3:12; 2 Cor. 5:21).[8]

What was the Holy Spirit saying to people about access to God through the arrangements of the Old Covenant? (Heb. 9:8)

What part of the human personality could the symbolism of the Old Covenant not reach? (Heb. 9:9)

WORD WEALTH

Conscience is the aspect of human personality that evaluates the morality of a person's behavior. "His 'conscience,' as the power directing this process, is regarded as apart from himself (Rom. ix.1; 11.15). The conscience may be imperfectly disciplined and informed (1 Cor. v.25 ff.; viii.7 ff. . . .). It may again be modified (1 Cor. viii.10, 12), and defiled (Tit. 1.15); and finally it may be seared and become insensible (1 Tim. iv.2). The man is responsible for the character which it assumes. . . .

"The absolute use of the word presents various functions which the conscience fulfils. It is a witness (2 Cor. 1.12; Rom. 11.15); a judge (2 Cor. iv.2; 5.11); a motive (1 Pet. ii.19; 1 Cor. x.25 ff.; Rom. xiii 5) It is tuned to God (Acts xxiii.1; xxiv.16); and it becomes an object of consideration to men (1 Cor. x.28 f.)."[9]

Why could the Old Covenant never perfect the human conscience? (Heb. 9:10)

What kind of purification from sin occurred in the symbolic system of the Old Covenant with its tabernacle worship? (Heb. 9:7, 9, 10)

WORD WEALTH

The Greek term translated **reformation** appears nowhere else in biblical Greek. It has the sense of "making straight." The word can mean either to correct what is defective or to replace the old with the new. The latter sense is the one in Hebrews 9:10. The expression "imposed until the time of reformation" implies that God always had intended the Old Covenant to be transitory.

 ### FAITH ALIVE

What would you find most frustrating about needing a priest to intercede with God on your behalf for all of your spiritual needs?

Which parts of the tabernacle arrangement and furnishings do you find meaningful as symbols about approaching God? Why?

REAL PURIFICATION

The New Covenant replaced the old one by fulfilling it. The New Covenant brought to light the realities that the old one symbolized. There is no competition between the two covenants. The new one replaced the old one like a Christmas present replaces its picture in the catalog. The present satisfies all the longings its picture aroused.

In two verses, the writer to the Hebrews quickly sketches the superior access to God provided through the High Priestly ministry of Christ (Heb. 9:11, 12). What is superior about each of these aspects of the ministry of Christ?

The covenant

The tabernacle

Access to God

Redemption

BEHIND THE SCENES

The Hebrew epistle contrasts the covenants of God through Moses and Christ. The Mosaic covenant provided animal sacrifices that brought temporary relief to man's guilt and demonstrated the lessons of God's justice. The covenant through Moses provided a bond in the blood of animals. The sacrifices, however, had to be repeated annually at the tabernacle, which was only symbolic of God's eternal, heavenly altar.

However, Jesus Christ came into history as an eternal Priest to offer an eternal sacrifice for sin. The shedding of His blood provided a permanent sacrifice and a permanent covenant between God and man. His Blood was applied not merely to an earthly altar, but to the very altar of God in heaven, where once and for all it obtained redemption from sin for those who receive Him. The immutable bond that is established through the New Covenant in Christ's blood is the ultimate fulfillment of God's covenant-making nature.[10]

When the writer of Hebrews said the Old Covenant sacrifices were "for the purifying of the flesh" (9:13), he did not mean cleaning the body. What kind of purification do you think the writer had in mind? Why use the term "flesh"?

According to Hebrews 9:14, describe the superior purification provided by the ministry of Christ according to each of these topics.

The sacrifice

The One who offered it

The extent of purification

The outcome of purification

 BIBLE EXTRA

The role of the Holy Spirit in the sacrifice of the Lord Jesus, alluded to in Hebrews 9:14, is not emphasized in the New Testament. The prophet Isaiah foresaw the entire life and ministry of the Messiah bathed in the power and direction of the Holy Spirit (1:2; 42:1; 48:16; 61:1). Among the Gospel writers, Luke stressed the empowering and sustaining role of the Spirit in and around the life of Jesus (1:15, 35; 2:25–27; 3:16, 22; 4:1, 14–21; 11:13; 12:8–12; Acts 1:2, 5, 8). Peter connected the Spirit with the resurrection of Jesus (1 Pet. 3:18).

How does the death of Christ both initiate the New Covenant and fulfill the Old Covenant? (Heb. 9:15)

BEHIND THE SCENES

Devotion is concentration on a particular pursuit, purpose, or cause. He who is devoted to Jesus recognizes his fleshly tendency to become lackadaisical and studies to avoid it. The Scriptures shape his thinking, and he devotes time to prayer, to waiting upon the Lord, and to praise and thanksgiving. Celebrate daily that you have gained access to God through the shed blood of Jesus Christ.[11]

FAITH ALIVE

How has Christ's Atonement purified your conscience?

What "dead works" have been removed from your life because of the purifying effect of Christ's Atonement?

What acts of service to God have replaced those dead works?

BASIS OF PURIFICATION

The Greek language of New Testament times used one word, *diatheke*, to cover the concepts we denote by the expressions "covenant" and "testament (will)." In the biblical world a death, either of a sacrifice or the testator, put the *diatheke* into effect. The writer of Hebrews includes both senses of *diatheke* in the next paragraph of chapter 9.

How did the death of Christ initiate the New Covenant? (Heb. 9:16, 17)

How was the Old Covenant initiated by death? (Heb. 9:18–21)

 BEHIND THE SCENES

"The Death of Christ fulfilled two distinct purposes. It provided an atonement for past sins; and, besides this, it provided an absolute ratification of the Covenant with which it was connected. . . .

"In any case a covenant is ratified by the death of a representative victim. But here Christ died in His own Person; and by thus dying He gave absolute validity to the covenant which He mediated."[12]

Why is blood so important to purification from sin? (Heb. 9:22; see Lev. 17:11; 1 Pet. 1:18, 19)

 WORD WEALTH

Remission comes from a root word meaning "to send away." The word signifies a release from bondage or imprisonment, dismissal, sending away, and forgiveness, with the added quality of canceling out all judgment, punishment, obligation, or debt.[13]

FAITH ALIVE

Write out as many promises as you can recall that God has guaranteed to you based on the covenant established by the death of Christ.

PURIFICATION IN HEAVEN

Exodus 24:3–8 recounts the ceremony in which Moses sprinkled blood on the Book of the Covenant and on the assembled congregation of Israel. The writer of Hebrews referred to that purification ceremony in Hebrews 9:18–20. In the next paragraph of the epistle, the writer turned to a corresponding ceremony in heaven.

Why would nothing less than the death of the Son of God suffice to purify the things of the New Covenant? (Heb. 9:23, 24)

How is Christ's entrance into the presence of God superior to the Levitical high priest's entrance into His presence on the Day of Atonement? (Heb. 9:24–26)

Why is it so important to the writer of Hebrews that Christ is now seated at the right hand of God? (Heb. 1:3; 8:1; 9:24–26)

Why do you think that the writer of Hebrews said that Christ died "at the end of the ages"? (Heb. 9:26)

How does the atoning death of Christ relate to the universal sentence of death and judgment awaiting all humans? (Heb. 9:27, 28)

WORD WEALTH

What would you like Christ to be doing on your behalf in the presence of the Father? (see 1 John 2:2)

1. Shakespeare, *Macbeth*, II,ii,35–37.
2. Ibid., 46, 47.
3. Ibid., 60–63.
4. Ibid., V,i,39, 40.
5. *Spirit-Filled Life Bible* (Nashville: Thomas Nelson Publishers, 1991), 137.
6. "Cherubim," *Nelson's Illustrated Bible Dictionary* (Nashville: Thomas Nelson Publishers, 1986), 217.
7. *Spirit-Filled Life Bible* (Nashville: Thomas Nelson Publishers, 1991), 1881, "Word Wealth: Hebrews 9:5, mercy seat."
8. "Feasts and Festivals," *Nelson's Illustrated Bible Dictionary* (Nashville: Thomas Nelson Publishers, 1986), 380.
9. Brooke Foss Westcott, *The Epistle to the Hebrews* (Grand Rapids: Wm. B. Eerdmans Publishing Company, 1970 rprt. of 1892 edition), 293.
10. *Spirit-Filled Life Bible* (Nashville: Thomas Nelson Publishers, 1991), 1881, "Kingdom Dynamics: Hebrews 9:12, Christ's Sacrifice, Permanent Relief."
11. Ibid., 1891, "Truth-in-Action through Hebrews."
12. Westcott, *The Epistle to the Hebrews*, 265.
13. *Spirit-Filled Life Bible*, 1882, "Word Wealth: Hebrews 9:22, remission."

Lesson 9/The Best Sacrifice for Sin (10:1–18)

When Ray Stedman pastored the Peninsula Bible Church in Palo Alto, California, he told the following story in a sermon based on the early verses of Hebrews 10: "I was born on the windswept plains of North Dakota. I remember as a boy sometimes seeing at night the flames of a prairie fire lighting the horizon, sweeping across the grass of those prairies. Such prairie fires were terrible threats to the pioneers who crossed the plains in their covered wagons. Often these fires would burn for miles and miles, threatening everything in their path.

"When they would see such a fire coming toward them, driven before the wind, they had a device they would use to protect themselves. They would simply light another fire and the wind would catch it up and drive it on beyond them and then they would get in the burned-over place and when the fire coming toward them reached it, it found nothing to burn and went out.

"God is saying that the cross of Jesus Christ is such a burned over place. Those who trust in it, and rest in the judgment that has already been visited upon it, have no other judgment to face."[1]

The perfection of the sacrifice of Jesus Christ is not aesthetic. Humanly speaking, His death was a brutal execution. Divinely speaking, His death was a sacrifice for sin, an offering that satisfied God's justice and at the same time expressed His passionate love and mercy for all, who would certainly be destroyed if God were only just and not also merciful (see Rom. 3:21–25). Stedman was wise to choose an analogy for the perfect death of Jesus that was unpleasant and terrifying.

SHADOW SACRIFICES

In Hebrews 9, the writer showed how the annual Day of Atonement under the terms of the Old Covenant foreshadowed the more excellent way into the presence of God that Christ opened by means of His death. In chapter 10, the writer of Hebrews turned his attention to the way the various sacrifices of the Old Covenant picture the infinite self-sacrifice of God's Son.

How did the writer of Hebrews contrast the nature of the Old Covenant with the nature of the New Covenant? (10:1)

 BEHIND THE SCENES

Law is an orderly system of rules and regulations by which a society is governed. In the Bible, particularly the Old Testament, a unique law code was established by direct revelation from God to direct His people in their worship, in their relationship to Him, and in their social relationships with one another.

Israel was not the only nation to have a law code. The biblical law code, or the Mosaic Law, was different from other ancient near eastern law codes in several ways. The biblical concept was that law comes from God, issues from His nature, and is holy, righteous, and good. Furthermore, at the outset of God's ruling over Israel at Sinai, God the great King gave His laws. These laws were binding on His people, and He upheld them. Furthermore, His laws were universal.

In Israel all crimes were crimes against God (1 Sam. 12:9, 10). Consequently, He expected all His people to love and serve Him (Amos 5:21–24). As the final judge, He disciplined those who violted His law (Ex. 22:21–24; Deut. 10:18; 19:17). The nation or community was responsible for upholding the law and insuring that justice was done (Deut. 13:6–10; 17:7; Num. 15:32–36).[2]

BEHIND THE SCENES

It is interesting that the writer of Hebrews compared the Old and New Covenants to "shadow" and "image" rather than to "shadow" and "reality." Historically interpreters have understood the writer to be using an image from the world of first-century art. The "shadow" is the sketch or outline, the plan for the painting. The "image" is the completed masterpiece, with all of the details and brilliant colors in place.

What do you think the writer meant by "the good things to come"? (Heb. 10:1; see 2:5; 6:5; 9:11; 13:14)

What were the shortcomings of the Old Covenant sacrifices in terms of each of these areas? (Heb. 10:1–4)

Repetition

Effect on worshiper

Efficacy of atonement

What kind of consciousness of sin would be created by the continual, steady repetition of Old Covenant sacrifices? (Heb. 10:2)

 BEHIND THE SCENES

Several different types of offerings are specified by God throughout the Old Testament. These demonstrate human need and God's merciful provision.

The burnt offering involved a male animal wholly consumed by fire. The animal was killed and the priest collected the blood and sprinkled it about the altar (Num. 28:1–8; see illustration). The burning symbolized the worshiper's desire to be purged of sinful acts. The meal offering, or grain offering, described in Leviticus 2 was similar in purpose to the burnt offering. The grain was brought to the priest, who threw a portion on the fire, accompanied by the burning of incense.

The peace offering was a ritual meal shared with God, the priests, and often other worshipers (Lev. 3). A voluntary animal offering, the sacrifice expressed praise to God and fellowship with others. Jacob and Laban offered this sacrifice when they made a treaty (Gen. 31:43–55). The sin offering, also known as the guilt offering, was offered to make atonement for sins for which restitution was not possible (Lev. 4:5–12). The trespass offering was made for lesser or unintentional offenses for which restitution was possible (Lev. 5:14–19).

The author of the Book of Hebrews identified Jesus as the great High Priest (Heb. 9:11) who replaced the system of animal sacrifices with a once-for-all sacrifice of Himself (Heb. 9:12–28). In the light of Christ's full and final offering for sin, Paul urged Christians "to present your bodies a living sacrifice" (Rom. 12:1).[2]

FAITH ALIVE

What kinds of repetitious behaviors do people nowadays sometimes count on to gain forgiveness for their sins?

Why can none such rituals produce forgiveness?

What kind of a new sacrifice should the inadequacies of the old sacrifices have caused worshipers to desire?

THE PERFECT SACRIFICE

You may be surprised by what the writer of Hebrews says about Jesus Christ as the perfect Sacrifice. The writer previously stressed the deity of Jesus (1:3) and the humanity of Jesus (2:14–18). He assumed all of that in chapter 10 before turning to Psalm 40 for an astonishing insight.

How has the writer of Hebrews earlier related the words of the psalmists to the words of Christ (or God)? (Heb. 10:5–7; see 1:5–9; 3:7–11; 5:5, 6; 8:8–12)

BEHIND THE SCENES

The writer of Hebrews quoted Psalm 40:6–8 from the Septuagint (often abbreviated as LXX), the Greek Old Testament, which was widely used because most Jews were more familiar with Greek than Hebrew. Read Psalm 40:6–8 and you discover that the second line says "My ears You have opened" instead of "But a body You have prepared for Me." The Septuagint translators seem to have interpreted David's words about his "ears" to mean that when his ears heard the truth about the true nature of sacrifices and offerings, he was ready to surrender his whole body in absolute, loving obedience. The open ears represented an obedient body.

If full atonement could not be made with animal sacrifices and cereal offerings, what needed to be offered? (Heb. 10:5)

If full atonement could not be achieved by the procedures of burnt offerings or sin offerings, what procedure must the new sacrifice follow? (Heb. 10:6, 7)

What effect did the words of Christ through David, the psalmist, produce relative to the Old and New Covenants? (Heb. 10:8, 9)

What was the will of God? (Heb. 10:10)

For Jesus Christ (see Heb. 10:5)

For us (see Heb. 2:11)

How would you relate the submission of Christ to the will of the Father and the lessons He learned through suffering? (Heb. 10:7, 9, 10; see 2:10; 5:8, 9)

WORD WEALTH

To sanctify is a major theological concept in the Book of Hebrews. The writer introduced it with the statement, "For both He who sanctifies and those who are being sanctified *are* all of one" (2:11). He will complete the concept by writing, "For by one offering He has perfected forever those who are being sanctified" (10:14).

In Hebrews sanctification has a different emphasis than in the writings of Paul, where the word captures the effect of the Holy Spirit on the character of a Christian. Here sanctification is the effect of Christ's atonement. The sacrifice of Christ completely "sets apart" the redeemed person for God.

FAITH ALIVE

God had far more in view than the rivers of blood that flowed on Jewish altars. What was He after? "Those sacrifices pointed to a human body in which there was a human will which continually chose to depend upon an indwelling God to obey a written Word! . . .

"When Christ came He paused on the threshold of heaven and said, 'A body thou hast prepared for me.' . . . That will in that human body never once acted on its own, never once took any step apart from dependence upon the Father who dwelt within."[3]

How does the attitude Jesus took into His sacrificial death compare to the attitude Paul commanded in Romans 12:1 for Christian living?

How many ways can you think of in which the first ten chapters of the Book of Hebrews has presented Christ as the perfect Sacrifice for your sins?

THE PERFECTING SACRIFICE

The most logical conclusion to draw about the effect of a sacrifice characterized by a body yielded to the will of God is that people saved because of it should yield their bodies to the will of God. Is that the conclusion the writer of Hebrews drew for his readers?

Contrast the old and new priestly ministries according to the following topics. (Heb. 10—12)

	OTHER PRIESTS	CHRIST
Sacrifice		
Frequency		
Effect		
Posture		

Hebrews 10:12 marks the third reference in the epistle to the seated position of Christ at God's right hand (see 1:3; 8:1). Why is it so important to the writer of Hebrews that Jesus is seated? Why do you think he alluded to Psalm 110:1 in Hebrews 10:13? (see Ps. 110:1–4)

WORD WEALTH

"Footstool" in Hebrews 10:13 creates a rich and important New Testament image based on Psalm 110:1. In the psalm, David wrote, "The LORD said to my Lord, 'Sit at My right hand, till I make Your enemies Your footstool.'" Jesus referred to this verse as evidence of His deity (Matt. 2:41–45; Mark 12:35–37; Luke 20:41–44). Peter did the same thing in his Pentecost sermon (Acts 2:34–36).

The writer of Hebrews used the reference to the footstool to highlight the idea that the work of Jesus is completed, and He sits at rest (Heb. 1:13; 10:1). In chapter 10 he added

the idea of waiting at rest for a time when evil will be van-
quished. The enemies of Christ will have to bow and let Him
put His feet on their necks as their Conqueror (see Josh.
10:24; 1 Kings 5:3).

Compare Hebrews 10:14 with 2:10, 11 and write down
what you think the writer means by being perfected and being
sanctified.

How does the blood of Jesus Christ relate to our being
sanctified (being both purified and related directly to God for
His work)? (see Eph. 2:11–22)

How does the Holy Spirit participate in our sanctification?
(2 Thess. 2:13)

WORD WEALTH

Perfected is a repeated word in Hebrews. The basic
meaning of the term is "mature" in the sense that a person
has arrived at the condition of life intended for him or her by
the will of God. In this sense Christ experienced perfecting
through His earthly existence (Heb. 2:10; 5:9; 7:28). Sinful
humans can know perfecting only through the transforming
work of the sacrifice of Christ (Heb. 6:1; 7:11, 19; 9:9; 10:14).
Perfection comes through a changed heart that surrenders its
will totally to the Father so the person behaves as a living
sacrifice (Rom. 12:1).

According to the Holy Spirit, what is the positive dimension of spiritual perfection? (Heb. 10:15, 16)

According to the Holy Spirit, what is the negative dimension of perfection? (Heb. 10:17)

What is the ultimate proof that Christ's sacrifice for sin never needs to be repeated? (Heb. 10:18)

FAITH ALIVE

What are the enemies of Christ you look forward to occuing subjected to Him? Why these?

What are the biggest hindrances to the perfection of your life as a living sacrifice whose will is continually submitted to the Father?

What Kingdom resources has God given us to overcome those hindrances? (2 Peter 1:3–4)

What assures us that God will continue transforming us unto Christlikeness? (Phil. 1:6, 2:13)

1. Ray Stedman, *What More Can God Say?* (Glendale, CA: Regal Books, 1974), 151. Used by permission.

2. "Old Testament Offerings," *The New Open Bible: Study Edition* (Nashville: Thomas Nelson Publishers, 1990), 121.

3. *What More Can God Say?* 154, 155.

Lesson 10/The Best Assurance of Salvation (10:19–39)

Childbirth is a strange and wonderful process. If you look at it one way, it's a violent, dangerous struggle for mother and child. From another perspective, it's a tender, heart-warming experience.

What assurance does a mother want when she faces childbirth? She doesn't expect to avoid pain and struggle. She expects both. She doesn't expect to avoid responsibility. She expects to take good care of herself and the unborn child. She doesn't expect the baby to arrive the day after she finds out she is pregnant. She expects to wait and put up with the inconveniences and discomforts of pregnancy.

The assurance the expectant mother wants is confidence that she will give birth to a healthy baby. If she has that assurance, then the responsibilities and risks become part of the process. They remind her that a healthy child is on its way. And if she has other children already, the memory of the responsibilities and risks assures her as well. These pains, these discomforts, these duties all mean that life is on its way.

The assurance of salvation in the Book of Hebrews is presented in a similar way. Spiritual life and growth has struggle and difficulty associated with it. Assurance of spiritual health does not depend on the absence of struggles with sin and the presence of warm, fuzzy feelings. Assurance should come from doing the duties, avoiding the perils, and treasuring the memories of past spiritual experiences.

THE ASSURANCE OF DUTIES DONE

When an expectant mother watches her diet, exercises carefully, and follows all of her doctor's instructions, she has assurance that her baby will develop in a healthy manner. The writer of Hebrews called on his readers to be assured of their salvation through active trust in Jesus Christ.

What ideas has the writer developed since the similar warning in Hebrews 4:14–16 that makes 10:19–22 more forceful?

BEHIND THE SCENES

"The Holiest" (Heb. 10:19; see 9:12) was the most sacred inner room in the tabernacle and the temple, where only the high priest was allowed to go. This room, separated from the rest of the worship area by a sacred veil, represented the visible presence of God in all His power and holiness. In this room was the ark of the covenant, covered by the sacred mercy seat (Ex. 25:10–22). Once a year on the Day of Atonement, the high priest entered the Most Holy Place with sacrificial blood and made atonement before God for the sins of the people (Leviticus 16).[1]

Circle in your Bible the two things the readers of Hebrews were reminded that they had (Heb. 10:19, 21) and underline the three things they were urged to do (vv. 22, 23, 24).

How did the flesh of Jesus make access to God the Father possible for those who believe in Him? (Heb. 10:19–22)

BIBLE EXTRA

Read the following passages about the veil in the tabernacle, then summarize its significance for biblical worship. Exodus 26:31–33; 40:17–21; Leviticus 4:1–21 (especially

vv. 6, 17); 16:1–34 (especially vv. 2, 12, 15); Numbers 4:5; 18:7; Matthew 27:50–54; Luke 23:44–49; 2 Corinthians 3:7–18; Hebrews 6:19, 20; 9:1–4; 10:20.

Literal significance

Symbolic significance

How are we to draw near to God? (Heb. 10:22)

Why should we be able to persevere in our Christian confession in spite of difficulties? (Heb. 10:23)

What behaviors should our consideration of one another as Christians lead to? (Heb. 10:24, 25)

How does the "let us" activity of Hebrews 10:22 lead logically to the "let us" of verse 23? How does the "let us" of verse 23 then lead to the "let us" of verses 24 and 25?

FAITH ALIVE

How can maintaining an active and vibrant daily relationship with Jesus Christ produce both the assurance of our salvation and the desire to perform our spiritual duties faithfully?

How have you found the corporate life of your church to be an aid in assurance of salvation?

THE ASSURANCE OF PERILS AVOIDED

An expectant mother who avoids the dangers of smoking and drinking gives herself assurance that her baby is developing nicely toward a healthy birth. On the other hand, the expectant mother who disregards all warnings in order to indulge herself is not just being careless. She loses her baby by despising it. She "apostatizes" from motherhood. To "sin willfully" (Heb. 10:26) is a more serious offense even than intentional backsliding. How is the concept of willful sinning expanded in verses 28 and 29?

How does each of these charges in Hebrews 10:29 accurately describe the actions of a believer in Christ who renounces his faith?

"Trampled the Son of God underfoot"

"Counted the blood of the covenant . . . a common thing"

"Insulted the Spirit of grace"

Why would the kind of repudiation of salvation described in Hebrews 10:29 leave one without "a sacrifice for sins"? (v. 26)

Most people who express concern about their salvation are troubled by nagging doubts. What is the spiritual expectation of the apostate? (Heb. 10:27)

How did the writer of Hebrews reason about the seriousness of the fate awaiting an apostate? (Heb. 10:28, 29)

What is the worst part of the judgment God has for an apostate member of His people? (Heb. 10:30, 31)

BEHIND THE SCENES

The writer of Hebrews had a particular scenario of apostasy in mind as he wrote his epistle. It would appear that the Jewish Christians to whom he wrote were considering reverting to the practice of Judaism in the face of persecution and ostracism by the larger Jewish community in which they lived. That is why the writer went to such trouble to develop biblical arguments for the temporary nature of the Old Covenant. The New Covenant in Christ is not just preferable. It has fulfilled and replaced the Old. One cannot go back without renouncing the only basis for the forgiveness of sins and eternal life.

 FAITH ALIVE

How would you distinguish doubt—even extreme doubt—from deliberate apostasy?

In what ways might Satan deceive a Christian to the point that he or she would renounce Christ?

Spiritual indifference and backsliding on the part of Christians are not the same thing as apostasy. How could these conditions put one in danger of choosing to apostatize?

In what way is struggling with doubt or struggling to achieve victory over sin an assurance of salvation rather than an evidence of apostasy?

THE ASSURANCE OF PRECIOUS MEMORIES

A woman who has successfully given birth before can comfort herself with memories of that earlier child's birth. Even if that labor unto birth was difficult, it serves as an assurance that the struggle is about life. Memories add perspective to the pressures of the moment that otherwise might take a mother's eyes off of the larger picture.

What had the Hebrew Christians experienced in the early days of their Christian life? (Heb. 10:32–34)

In persecution

In supporting the persecuted

In material loss

 WORD WEALTH

Illuminated (Heb. 10:32) translates a Greek verb that occurs here and in Hebrews 6:4. The image pictures the moment when the truth of Christ was apprehended by the human mind and spirit and accepted by faith. That moment of insight and faith was like a light being lit. The same moment of conversion is described in 10:26 with the expression "received the knowledge of the truth."

 WORD WEALTH

Struggle (Heb. 10:32) translates the Greek noun *athlesis,* from which English derives the word athletics. The basic meaning of the word is "contest," but metaphorically it easily means "fight" or "struggle." The notion is that the Hebrew Christians once had successfully "endured a great struggle with sufferings." Like good athletes, they were encouraged to continue to endure so that, after they had done the will of God, they might "receive the promise" (Heb. 10:36).

How had the Hebrew Christians been able to endure their earlier period of persecution? (Heb. 10:34)

How does the appeal in Hebrews 10:35 relate to the warning about apostasy in verses 26–31?

 WORD WEALTH

Confidence (Heb. 10:35) stresses the "boldness" that had belonged to the Hebrew Christians in the past (same word in 4:16 and 10:19). A different word in Hebrews 3:14 adds the dimension of firm resolve also needed in "confidence."

Even as Jesus persevered in doing the will of God (Heb. 10:5–10), so believers in Jesus also need to persevere (v. 36). What is the reward of persevering in the will of God? (Heb. 10:36, 37)

 WORD WEALTH

Endurance (Heb. 10:36) means constancy, perseverance, continuance, bearing up, steadfastness, holding out, patient endurance. The word combines *hupo,* "under," and *mone,* "to remain." It describes the capacity to continue to bear up under difficult circumstances, not with a passive complacency, but with a hopeful fortitude that actively resists weariness and defeat.[2]

What is the means of persevering in the will of God? (Heb. 10:38)

 BEHIND THE SCENES

Habakkuk was an Old Testament prophet who struggled with the problem of evil. First, he could not understand why God did not punish His covenant people for their sin. Later, he could not reconcile God's punishment of sinful Judah by means of grossly wicked Babylon. Finally, Habakkuk abandoned his struggle by trusting in the righteous character of God. He trusted that God was just; that He would ultimately judge sin fairly. If he had to suffer in the meantime, he would do so trusting the Lord to make things right in the end.

"For the vision is yet for an appointed time;
But at the end it will speak, and it will not lie.
Though it tarries, wait for it;
Because it will surely come,
It will not tarry.
Behold the proud,
His soul is not upright in him;
But the just shall live by his faith."
—Habakkuk 2:3, 4

Why did the writer of Hebrews contrast those who "draw back to perdition" and those who "believe to the saving of the soul"? (Heb. 10:39)

FAITH ALIVE

What memories do you have from earlier in your Christian life when you endured opposition for your faith in Christ?

How do your memories motivate you to belong to the people of faith rather than to those who draw back to perdition?

How do your memories add to your assurance of salvation?

1. "Holy Place," *Nelson's Illustrated Bible Dictionary* (Nashville: Thomas Nelson Publishers, 1986), 486.

2. *Spirit-Filled Life Bible* (Nashville: Thomas Nelson Publishers, 1991), 1884, "Word Wealth: Hebrews 10:36, endurance."

Lesson 11/The Best Object of Faith (11:1–40)

Thomas Hardy wrote a novel entitled *Jude the Obscure*. Perhaps he should have called it *Habakkuk the Obscure*, for certainly the minor prophet Habakkuk is much more obscure than Jude. But I don't suppose Hardy could have done that, because, while Jude is an unusual name, Habakkuk is a name no one used, even long ago when Old Testament names were in vogue.

The Lord gave Habakkuk an unpleasant task as a prophet. He got to tell the nation of Judah that they were wicked enough that God was going to punish them by means of the Babylonians who were ten times worse. Habakkuk was convinced that God had made a moral error in deciding to punish the bad by means of the worse, and told Him so. When the Lord failed to change His mind, Habakkuk did some serious soul searching.

As a result of his inner struggle Habakkuk, the prophet with the goofy name, reached a staggering conclusion—a conclusion that shaped all of the theology of Paul and later all of the Reformation of Martin Luther. Habakkuk said, "The just shall live by his faith" (Hab. 2:4). And to show that he knew what he was prophesying about, Habakkuk ended his prophecy with this prayer:

> Though the fig tree may not blossom,
> Nor fruit be on the vines;
> Though the labor of the olive may fail,
> And the fields yield no food;
> Though the flock may be cut off from the fold,
> And there be no herd in the stalls —
> Yet I will rejoice in the LORD,
> I will joy in the God of my salvation.
> The LORD God is my strength;

He will make my feet like deer's feet,
And He will make me walk on my high hills.
—Habakkuk 3:17–19

Hebrews 10:37 and 38 quoted Habakkuk 2:3 and 4. The writer of Hebrews then devoted the longest chapter of the epistle to the importance of faith in Christ to his readers who were struggling with the temptation to revert to their former Jewish religion.

FAITH AND REALITY

The first seven verses of Hebrews 11 describe faith and illustrate how faith in God and His Word provide a basic framework for understanding and dealing with reality.

What do you think is the difference in meaning between "things hoped for" and "things not seen"? (Heb. 11:1)

The word "substance" has the idea of foundation or basis. The word "evidence" has the idea of test or proof. How do you think faith provides a foundation or basis "of things hoped for"? (Heb. 11:1)

How do you think faith provides a test or proof "of things not seen"? (Heb. 11:1)

AT A GLANCE

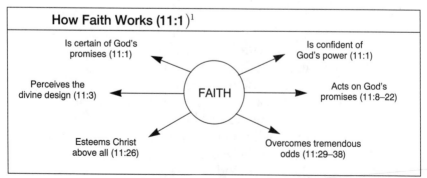

How Faith Works (11:1)[1]

Is certain of God's promises (11:1)

Is confident of God's power (11:1)

Perceives the divine design (11:3)

FAITH

Acts on God's promises (11:8–22)

Esteems Christ above all (11:26)

Overcomes tremendous odds (11:29–38)

The remainder of Hebrews 11 traces how various Old Testament characters and many anonymous saints trusted God regarding "things hoped for" and "things not seen" (v. 2). The writer wanted his readers to determine to imitate this faith.

BEHIND THE SCENES

The elders (Heb. 11:2) were the Old Testament saints, many of whom are mentioned in this chapter. They obtained a good report, not because of achievements, personal holiness, or passive acceptance of divine promises, but by an active certitude expressed in obedience, persistence, and sacrifice.[2]

What aspects of faith's role in grasping reality is illustrated by each of these Old Testament incidents?

Creation (Heb. 11:3)

Abel's sacrifice (Heb. 11:4)

Enoch's translation (Heb. 11:5, 6)

Noah's ark (Heb. 11:7)

FAITH ALIVE

"This chapter centers on and focuses upon what faith is. . . . It might help to show, first of all, what faith is not. Faith, for instance, is not positive thinking; that is something quite different. Faith is not a hunch that is followed. Faith is not hoping for the best, hoping that everything will turn out all right. Faith is not a feeling of optimism. Faith is none of these things though all of them have been identified as faith. . . .

"Faith is believing there is another dimension to life other than those which can be touched, tasted, seen or felt. . . . Faith believes that God, in His grace, has stepped over the boundary into human history and told us some great and very valuable facts. Faith believes them and adjusts its life to those facts and walks on that basis."[3]

How do Christ and His work fit into the category of things hoped for and things not seen?

Why do you think God values your faith (Heb. 1:6) more than any other attitude you can direct toward Him?

Which area of reality illustrated in Hebrews 11:3–7 would you like to see strengthened in your spiritual understanding? Why?

FAITH AND PROMISE

When faith turns from foundational issues of reality to personal issues of salvation, people find out whether they trust God to make and keep His promises with them. It's one thing to believe that God has established a physical, moral, and spiritual order in the universe. It's another matter to believe that He wants to direct my life, and still another for me to let Him direct my life.

According to Hebrews 11:8–12, how did Abraham trust God to keep His promises to him in each of these areas?

His destination

His place

His posterity

How do Hebrews 11:10 and 12 illustrate the basic description of faith given in verse 1?

What is the universal confession of men and women of faith? (Heb. 11:13–16)

BEHIND THE SCENES

Faith's Confession Is Steadfast (Heb. 11:13–16). This chapter records glorious victories of faith's champions, yet vv. 13–16 speak of those who died, "not having received the promises." Even then, the Bible says "these all died in faith," being content to confess that they were only strangers and pilgrims traveling, as it were, through the land: "For true believers, to live by faith is to die by faith" (Wycliffe).

The key to the "confession" (v. 13) of this admirable group in Hebrews 11 is that when given a promise by God, as were Abraham and his descendants, they became "fully persuaded" that the promise was true. Thus they embraced (literally "greeted") that promise in their hearts. The word "confess" helps us to understand how easily these of the gallery of faith established their ways before God and left the testimony, which His Word records with tribute.

While each of these persons did receive *many* victories through faith, the text says that none of them received *everything* that was promised. Whether or not we receive what we "confess" (ask, pray, or hope for) does not change the behavior or attitude of the steadfast believer. Faith's worship and walk do not depend on answered or unanswered prayers. Our confession of His lordship in our lives is to be consistent—a daily celebration, with deep gratitude.[4]

What would Hebrews 11:13–16 mean to first-century Hebrew Christians considering abandoning faith in Christ and returning to their former Jewish religion?

 BEHIND THE SCENES

Although they received only a partial fulfillment of what God had promised, these elders maintained their faith that God would do what He said. Because of their close relationship with God, they could not feel at home in earthly surroundings. They looked for something better; and because of their longings, God gladly acknowledged them as His own people.[5]

In Hebrews 11:17–22, how did each of these patriarchs of Israel demonstrate faith as "the substance of things hoped for, the evidence of things not seen"? (v. 1)

Abraham

Isaac

Jacob

Joseph

How did the promises of God as the object of the patriarchal faith distinguish their faith from wishful thinking or blind optimism?

WORD WEALTH

The Greek word translated **promise** *(epangelia)* differs by only one letter from the word translated gospel *(euangelia)*. While the "gospel" is a good and pleasant announcement from God, the "promise" is a sure and certain announcement from God. In Hebrews "the promise" is synonymous with the New Covenant or testament by which people of faith inherit the purification of sanctification. The promise is established through the High Priestly ministry of Jesus on the basis of His once-for-all sacrifice of Himself for sins.

FAITH ALIVE

What promises of God make your saving faith and daily faith more than wishful thinking and blind optimism?

How are faith in the Person of Christ and faith in the promises of God related to one another?

FAITH AND VICTORY

Faith perceives what is real, and faith grasps the promises of God that bring His blessings to bear on the believer's life. Furthermore, faith is the basis for all victories in the conflicts and conquests of the spiritual life.

According to Hebrews 11:23–31, how did faith at each stage in the following sequence contribute to the redemption of Israel and the conquest of Canaan?

The concealment of infant Moses

Moses' identification with Israel

The Exodus from Egypt

The conquest of Jericho

 BEHIND THE SCENES

If Moses had remained in the court of Pharaoh rather than identifying with the people of Israel, he would have become a man of great worldly power. He had received the finest education of the day and demonstrated unusual ability as an orator and leader (Acts 7:22). In time Moses would have distinguished himself as a well-known man in the mightiest empire of the world—and been lost in the obscurity of history.

Instead Moses regarded such a choice as sin against the will of God (Heb. 11:25). He lay aside his claim to fame and power to obey God's call with a bunch of slaves. In the process, he became one of the most famous and influential men who ever lived. He was the friend of God (Ex. 33:11) and the inspired author of the first five books of the Old Testament.

What would the choice of Moses to suffer affliction mean to Hebrew Christians considering rejecting their faith in Christ to avoid affliction? (Heb. 11:25, 26)

WORD WEALTH

Looked (Heb. 11:26) is a graphic word combining *apo*, "away from," and *blepo*, "to see." The word literally means "to look away from everything else in order to look intently on one object." Moses looked away from the wealth of the world systems toward a messianic future.[6]

Why was it necessary for faith to see "Him who is invisible" when Moses was facing "the wrath of the king"? (Heb. 11:27)

Why do you think Rahab was such a good example of someone who exercised faith as "the substance of things hoped for, the evidence of things not seen" as a means to victory? (Heb. 11:31; see Josh. 2:8–14)

FAITH ALIVE

How has your faith in Christ already given you victory over sin, death, and the world?

What do you need to look away from in order to keep looking in faith toward the Lord Jesus and the Word of God?

FAITH AND CONFLICT

The Hebrew Christians who received this epistle were experiencing conflict because of their faith in Jesus. It was uncertain whether they would experience victory over their persecutors. In fact, it was much more likely that the persecution would continue indefinitely.

According to Hebrews 11:32–35a, what sorts of achievements against overwhelming odds did judges, kings, and prophets in ancient Israel experience in these areas?

Spiritual achievements

Heroic deeds

Personal accomplishments

According to Hebrews 11:35b–38, what sorts of achievements against overwhelming odds did a multitude of anonymous Old Testament heroes achieve through faith?

Those who died

Those who survived

 BEHIND THE SCENES

The fact that others were tortured and suffered in various other ways indicates that faith does not provide an automatic exemption from hardship, trials, or tragedy. Furthermore, the experience of such difficulties does not mean that the people undergoing them possess less faith than those who are not afflicted. The same faith that enables some to escape trouble enables others to endure it. The same faith that delivers some from death enables others to die victoriously.

Faith is not a bridge over troubled waters, but is a pathway through them. Discerning the pathway and the source of any hardships encountered requires aggressive prayer and worship. Through these means, God's perspective becomes focused.[7]

What would this catalog of suffering and death have meant to the Hebrew Christian recipients of this epistle who were considering apostatizing from their faith in Jesus?

According to Hebrews 11:39 and 40, what were the accomplishments of the heroes of faith?

Relative to their reputations

Relative to God's promise

Relative to the Hebrew Christians

Why do you think the faithful saints of the Old Covenant need the company of the faithful saints of the New Covenant to be perfect? (Heb. 1:40)

FAITH ALIVE

How can your faith in Christ—who is the best object of faith—sustain you through times of persecution?

What worldly attitudes do you need to deal with to give your faith freedom to resist persecution?

Who have you known that was a person of such faith that "the world was not worthy" of him or her? How did he or she show this faith?

1. *The Wesley Bible* (Nashville: Thomas Nelson Publishers, 1991), 1858.
2. *Spirit-Filled Life Bible* (Nashville: Thomas Nelson Publishers, 1991), 1884, note on Hebrews 11:2.
3. Ray Stedman, *What More Can God Say?* (Glendale, CA: Regal Books, 1974), 182, 192. Used by permission.
4. *Spirit-Filled Life Bible*, 1885, 1886, "Kingdom Dynamics: Hebrews 11:13–16, Faith's Confession Is Steadfast."
5. Ibid., 1885, note on Hebrews 11:13–16.
6. Ibid., 1886, "Word Wealth: Hebrews 11:26, looked."
7. Ibid., 1887, note on Hebrews 11:35–38.

Lesson 12/The Best Way to Follow Jesus
(12:1–29)

Little Mikey was a surprise to his parents—a fifth child born when the other four were teenagers. Mom and Dad's future plans had not included diapers and sleepless nights. They had struggled for years to make an earth-moving business profitable, and finally achieved some prosperity after focusing on the demolition of old buildings in decaying neighborhoods.

Based on that success Mikey's parents had bought a farm with magnificent nineteenth-century buildings. The brick house on the hill had solid masonry interior walls and vaulted chambers in the basement where crops and livestock had been kept. The glass in the ancient windows was all original—filled with runs and bubbles that distorted the vistas of fields and woods.

When he was four years old, Mikey took a baseball bat and walked around the outside of his mother's dream home and shattered every pane of century-old glass he could reach from the ground. His mother flew at him in a blind rage, about to do violence to her darling when the light dawned about this strange act of destruction.

You see, Mikey went almost everyday with his father out on job sites. Workmen passed him around and took turns keeping an eye on him while they cut interior load-bearing supports, collapsed the structure, and hauled away the debris. But before the men did anything else to a building, they took lengths of boards or pipes and broke out all the glass, so there would be no fragments flying around when the walls and roof caved in.

Breaking windows had always looked like fun to Mikey, and it was what he had figured Daddy did for a living. You can't exactly punish a kid for trying to follow in his father's footsteps.

The writer of Hebrews held up Jesus as the example for the Hebrew Christians to follow as they tried to decide how to handle the hostility they were experiencing because of their faith. The Hebrews needed more maturity in their imitation of Jesus than Mikey displayed in imitating his father, but they needed the same enthusiasm and energy.

ACCEPT DISCIPLINE

Most imitation begins with a burst of zeal or idealism. The writer of Hebrews knew that his readers had once felt that ardor (10:32–34). Now they needed a quality to their imitation of Jesus that could carry them through their entire lives.

Who do you think make up the "cloud of witnesses," and what is their function in the writer's metaphor of the race? (Heb. 12:1)

What does the writer encourage his readers to do to run the race successfully? (Heb. 12:1, 2)

Negatively

Positively

What characteristics make Jesus the best example of how to run the race of the Christian life in the face of persecution? (Heb. 12:2)

How do you think careful contemplation of the hostility Jesus suffered will prevent discouragement on the part of persecuted Christians? (Heb. 12:3)

 BEHIND THE SCENES

How to Develop Dynamic Discipleship (Heb. 12:1–11). The disciple is an apprentice to Jesus, learning to live as He did. Discard any attitude or practice that hinders your walk with Christ. Model your life after Jesus. Give careful thought and study to the life of Jesus for encouragement in your struggle with sin. Embrace God's discipline. Know that it is evidence that He is training you as His child. Accept God's correction as necessary for spiritual growth.[1]

The Hebrew Christians were in danger of being overwhelmed by their persecutions. When they compared their sufferings with those of Jesus, what two things did they need to remember?

As a matter of fact (Heb. 12:4)

As a matter of exhortation (Heb. 12:5, 6; see Prov. 3:10, 11)

What does the presence or absence of difficulty in life suggest about one's Father-child relationship with God? (Heb. 12:7, 8)

According to Hebrews 12:9 and 10, how did the writer contrast our earthly fathers and our heavenly Father?

	EARTHLY FATHERS	HEAVENLY FATHER
Response to		
Motivation		

What is the outcome of painful discipline for Jesus and for His followers?

For Jesus (Heb. 12:2)

For His followers (Heb. 12:11)

BEHIND THE SCENES

The readers must not assume that the sufferings they are enduring as a result of their Christian profession mean that God is unconcerned about their welfare. Far from neglecting them, He shows Himself to be a true Father in the experience of discipline.

"Chastens" describes corrective discipline used in training a child. Such treatment is administered not harshly, but in love, with the well-being of the child in mind. Instead of becoming discouraged, the readers should view their persecutions as evidence of God's love for them as His children, bringing them to spiritual maturity.

The writer does not suggest that God is responsible for the sufferings that hostile sinners bring upon them, but he does indicate that God uses even adverse circumstances as instruments to accomplish His purpose.[2]

 FAITH ALIVE

What encouragement do you or could you derive from the witness of biblical heroes of faith and heroes of faith from church history?

What disciplines do you need in order to become a better follower and imitator of Jesus?

Physically

Emotionally

Socially

Economically

Spiritually

DEVELOP STRENGTH

Before you can follow the example of Jesus successfully for any length of time, you need to build up your spiritual vitality and purity. A lot of fans watch sporting contests religiously and imagine themselves performing the feats their favorite players do, but in reality they are in no physical condition to do any of it. Spiritually we can marvel at the grace and truth of Jesus and not have the spiritual conditioning to imitate Him.

In terms of persevering in a literal footrace, what is the meaning of the commands in Hebrews 12:12, 13?

In terms of persevering in the race of the spiritual life, what is the meaning of the commands in Hebrews 12:12, 13?

In the face of persecution and amid a life of discipline, what should a spiritually strong person's life be like? (Heb. 12:14)

In relation to other people

In relation to God

What three dangers must a strong Christian avoid, and why do you think he or she must avoid them? (Heb. 12:15, 16)

	DANGER	REASON TO AVOID IT
1		
2		
3		

WORD WEALTH

Root of bitterness is an allusion to Deuteronomy 29:18 where the "root of bitterness" is a person who defiles the believing community by worshiping false gods. In Hebrews 12:15, the "root of bitterness" seems to be an attitude that contrasts with being at peace with all people (v. 14). A bitter attitude is an unforgiving spirit that blames others for one's troubles and causes divisions within a family, neighborhood, or church.

BEHIND THE SCENES

The fate of Esau (Heb. 12:16, 17) serves as a solemn warning to anyone who forfeits permanent spiritual blessings for immediate passing fleshly gratification. Once such a choice is made and acted on, its consequences cannot be reversed, and the blessings that might have been realized are lost forever.[3]

Esau was a son of Isaac and Rebekah and the twin brother of Jacob. Esau was born first. By Old Testament custom, he would have inherited most of his father's property and the right to succeed him as family patriarch. But in a foolish, impulsive moment, he sold his birthright to Jacob in exchange for a meal (Gen. 25:29–34).

Esau in many ways was more honest and dependable than his scheming brother Jacob. But he sinned greatly by treating his birthright so casually and selling it for a meal. To the ancient Hebrews, one's birthright actually represented a high spiritual value. But Esau did not have the faith and far-sightedness to accept this privilege and responsibility. Thus, the right passed by default to his younger brother.[4]

   FAITH ALIVE

What practical steps could you take to strengthen your Christian life?

What practical steps could you take to remove from your life the characteristics warned against in Hebrews 12:15 and 16?

What practical steps can you take to assist your Christian brothers and sisters to become stronger saints?

RESPECT HOLINESS

Following Jesus is like running a relay race. He ran the first leg and showed how to surrender one's body and life to do the will of the Father. It takes discipline and strength to accept the baton for one's own leg of the race. It also requires a consciousness that the race of life is being run in service to the holy God of the universe. This is not a game.

What was it like when the Lord appeared at Mount Sinai to establish the Old Covenant with Israel through Moses? (Heb. 12:18–21)

 BEHIND THE SCENES

The trumpet blown at Mount Sinai was a *shophar* made of a ram's horn. The *shophar* was the greatest of the Jewish ritual instruments. It was basically a signaling instrument, used to assemble the army (Judg. 3:27; 1 Sam. 13:3), to sound an attack (Job 39:24, 25), and to sound an alarm (Jer. 6:1; Amos 3:6).

The *shophar* signaled war and peace, the new moon, the beginning of the Sabbath, approaching danger, and the death of a dignitary. The sound of the trumpet could be heard from a great distance (Ex. 19:16, 19). It can produce only the first two tones of the musical scale and those not very accurately. The ram's horn is seldom mentioned with other musical instruments. Its main function was to make noise.[5]

What majesty and glory accompany a person's entrance into the New Covenant? (Heb. 12:22–24)

Regarding the location of the ceremony

Regarding the participants in the ceremony

Regarding the sacrifice in the ceremony

The Israelites while at Mount Sinai waiting for Moses were ready to return to Egypt and to worship idols. The Hebrew Christians to whom this epistle was sent were contemplating returning to the Jewish religion. Why did the writer of Hebrews advise against refusing the covenant they had entered with God? (Heb. 12:25–27)

 BEHIND THE SCENES

Restoration and the Shaking of Man's Works (Heb. 12:26, 27). Everything Israel and Judah built up in generations of self-effort was an abomination to God, and He systematically gave over for destruction all they had accomplished by "the works of their own hands" (Jer. 1:16; 32:29–36).

The message of their misconception speaks to us today, and the [writer of Hebrews] summarizes the shaking God is determined to perform (Heb. 12:26, 27). Everything built by the hand of man, in the energy and wisdom of the flesh, He has vowed to shake down. Only the things that cannot be shaken—the things built in His eternal power and wisdom—will remain.

The great shaking [the author of Hebrews] prophesied has begun and is continuing in the church today. For the same evils that plagued Israel—seeking to please God by external performance, lapsing into idolatry and moral decay, corruption in leadership, and worshiping the works of men's hands—are too present even in the church. Their removal is an essential part of the restoration process.

To the church as a whole, restoration means more than becoming a reproduction of the New Testament church. It means becoming all God originally intended the church to be. Remember, restoration means the establishment of something more and better than the original.[6]

At some point in the future, God will shake the heavens and earth in judgment (Heb. 12:26, 27). What does it mean to you that these things are eternal and unshakable? (v. 28)

God's kingdom

God's grace

Our service to God

Reverence and godly fear

What security is provided by the unshakable elements of Hebrews 12:28 when dealing with a holy God who "*is* a consuming fire"? (Heb. 12:29; see Ex. 24:17)

FAITH ALIVE

Why is it important to revere the holiness and majesty of God while imitating and following Jesus?

How can a sense of the majesty and terrible power of your holy God give you confidence to face opposition?

1. *Spirit-Filled Life Bible* (Nashville: Thomas Nelson Publishers, 1991), 1892, "Truth-in-Action through Hebrews."

2. Ibid., 1887, note on Hebrews 12:5–11.

3. Ibid., 1888, note on Hebrews 12:16, 17.

4. "Esau," *Nelson's Illustrated Bible Dictionary* (Nashville: Thomas Nelson Publishers, 1986), 350, 351.

5. "Musical Instruments," Ibid., 737.

6. "The Holy Spirit and Restoration," *Spirit-Filled Life Bible*, 2014, 2017.

Lesson 13/The Best Shepherd (13:1–25)

When J. R. R. Tolkien wrote his fantasy stories about hobbits and Middle Earth, he revealed his love of trees. Some of Tolkien's best descriptions are of massive trees deep in primeval forests. Eventually Tolkien created a group of creatures he called "ents." "Ents" were the shepherds of the trees.

An ent looked like the trunk of a tree with shortened branches and roots. An ent walked on its "roots" and used its "branches" as arms. Most of the time the ents stood motionless in the depths of the forest watching over their trees to protect them from harm and tend them so that they flourished.

In Tolkien's scheme of things, the ents were patient and wise. They lived enormous spans of time and changed little. Animals and men who passed through the forest had no notion of the presence of the ents. They seemed to be ancient tree trunks surviving among the living, younger wood. But the ents saw all the creatures and marked who was friend and who was foe to the trees.

And some day a time would come when the ents would waken the trees from their drowsy state to a fuller life. It might take eons, but the ents would shepherd until their presence among the trees had transformed them.

Tolkien's tale of trees and ents is a pleasant feature in the second volume of *The Lord of the Rings* for anyone who loves the forest. Ents suggest something of the shepherding ministry of the Lord Jesus in the lives of Christians. But Jesus is the Good Shepherd who lay down His life for the sheep. There is no other shepherd like Him in that regard.

THE PRESENCE OF THE SHEPHERD

Hebrews 13 stands a bit apart from the rest of the epistle. The writer's planned presentation ended with the final words of chapter 12, and the final chapter presents a collection of parting thoughts, a benediction, and personal greetings. The first portion involves conduct prompted and enabled by the presence of the Lord in our lives.

How did the writer of Hebrews instruct believers to show brotherly love (Heb. 13:1) in the following situations?

Hospitality (Heb. 13:2)

Treatment of prisoners (Heb. 13:3)

   WORD WEALTH

Brotherly love translates the Greek word *philadelphia* (which is why Philadelphia, Pennsylvania, is called "The City of Brotherly Love"). The Greek term is compounded from *phileo,* "to love," and *adelphos,* "brother." The love denoted by *phileo* is affection based on natural attraction. The brotherhood created by faith in Jesus as Savior and Lord should bind believer to believer in warm, affectionate friendships based on Jesus' name.

BEHIND THE SCENES

Imprisonment in biblical times differed in purpose from imprisonment in modern western societies. Imprisonment was not used as punishment for criminal behavior. Various forms of harsh corporal punishment typically punished crimes. In a few cases imprisonment removed troublesome people from society because civil authorities found their opinions or presence created social unrest. Long-term prisoners were, therefore, usually prisoners of conscience (for example, John the Baptist).

The vast majority of prisoners were being detained prior to trial or punishment (for example, Peter in Acts 12 and Paul and Silas in Acts 16). A debtor might be imprisoned until he was sold as a slave in order to pay his debts (Matt. 18:25, 30).

Imprisoned Christians, therefore, were probably short-term detainees in primitive dungeons or cells (see Acts 12:6; 16:24) facing trial and physical punishment. They might need clothing (see 2 Tim. 4:13), medical attention, and better food as well as personal and spiritual support.

How should the presence of the Lord as Shepherd affect the attitude of Christians toward marriage and sexual behavior? (Heb. 13:4)

BEHIND THE SCENES

In order to guard against sexual immorality, God has ordained the sacred relationship of marriage. "Undefiled" contains more than an approval of conjugal relationship, but also entails the married couple's responsibility to preserve their intimacy from the perverse and debasing practices of a lewd society.[1]

How should the presence of the Lord as Shepherd affect the attitude of Christians toward material possessions? (Heb. 13:5)

How does the quotation of Psalm 118:6 (from the Greek Old Testament, the Septuagint) by the writer of Hebrews provide a spiritual basis for boldness to obey the instruction of Hebrews 13:1–5? (Heb. 13:6)

 WORD WEALTH

Helper translates *boethos,* which is compounded of *boe,* "a cry for help" and *theo,* "to run." *Boethos* is one who comes running when we cry for help. The word describes the Lord as poised and ready to rush to the relief of His oppressed children when they shout for His assistance.[2]

 FAITH ALIVE

How can you better express brotherly love within the body of Christ, especially in the area of being hospitable and caring for the imprisoned?

In what area of your spiritual life would you like to see the help of God produce an improvement in response to your outcry?

THE STABILITY OF THE SHEPHERD

Hebrews 13:1–6 shows how the presence of the Shepherd produces harmony and contentment among the sheep. Verses 7–17 deal with the stability the Shepherd creates by various means for His flock.

The Shepherd provides leaders to represent Him to the rest of the flock. What does the Shepherd expect from His flock as a means toward stability? (Heb. 13:7, 17)

The leaders

The followers

How should the nature of the Shepherd provide doctrinal stability for His flock? (Heb. 13:8, 9)

How did the self-sacrifice of the Shepherd set apart His flock from the followers of the Old Covenant? (Heb. 13:10–12)

BEHIND THE SCENES

An altar was a table or elevated surface on which a priest placed a sacrifice as an offering to God. The first altar in the Bible was the one built by Noah after the Flood (Gen. 8:20). The next several altars mentioned appear in connection with the patriarch Abraham and his wanderings (Gen. 12:7, 8; 13:18; 22:9). To these altars, his son Isaac added one at Beersheba (Gen. 26:25). Isaac's son Jacob built no new altars; but he restored those which Abraham had built at Shechem (Gen. 33:20) and Bethel (Gen. 35:1, 3).

The Hebrew word for altar means "a place of slaughter or sacrifice." But the altars of the Old Testament were not restricted to offerings of animals as sacrifices. Joshua 22:26–29 indicates that altars were occasionally used to remind the Israelites of their heritage or to call attention to a major event. Sometimes an altar might even be used as a place of refuge (1 Kin. 1:50, 51; 2:28).

During the days of Moses, two priestly altars assumed important roles in the ritual of the tabernacle in the wilderness. These were the altar of burnt offering and the altar of incense.[3]

How did the sacrifice of the Shepherd provide the Hebrew Christians with the necessary stability to resist the pressures to return to the practices of the Old Covenant? (Heb. 13:13, 14)

What sacrifices does the Shepherd want from His sheep in grateful response to His sacrifice for sins? (Heb. 13:15, 16)

BEHIND THE SCENES

The Sacrifice of Praise (Heb. 13:10–15). Why is praising God a sacrifice? The word "sacrifice" (Greek *thusia*) comes from the root *thuo,* a verb meaning "to kill or slaughter for a purpose." Praise often requires that we "kill" our pride, fear, or sloth—anything that threatens to diminish or interfere with our worship of the Lord.

We also discover here the basis of all our praise: the sacrifice of our Lord Jesus Christ. It is by Him, in Him, with Him, to Him, and for Him that we offer our sacrifice of praise to God. Praise will never be successfully hindered when we keep its focus on Him—the Founder and the Completer of our salvation. His Cross, His Blood—His love gift of life and forgiveness to us—keep praise as a *living* sacrifice![4]

FAITH ALIVE

How do you think leaders and followers in your church can better create the stability Jesus Christ, the Shepherd, wants for His people?

How do you think the Lord expects you to "go forth to Him, outside the camp, bearing His reproach"? (Heb. 13:13)

How can you improve your sacrifices to the Lord?

Sacrifices of praise

Sacrifices of doing good and sharing

 BIBLE EXTRA

Hebrews 13:20 and 21 presents Christ acting as the Great High Priest in response to the God of peace. Review the teaching of the Epistle to the Hebrews about Christ as High Priest. Look up the following passages and summarize them in the spaces provided.

I. The Heart of His High Priesthood

Hebrews 2:17, 18   *Made like us to become merciful & suffered & tempted faithful*

Hebrews 3:1, 2   *faithful*

Hebrews 4:14–16   *sympathize with weakness like us tempted not sinned*

II. The Characteristics of His High Priesthood

Hebrews 5:1–10

Hebrews 6:20; 7:14–19

Hebrews 7:26–28

III. The Word of His High Priesthood

Hebrews 8:1–6

Hebrews 9:11–28

Hebrews 10:1–18

IV. The Experience of His High Priesthood

Hebrews 10:19–25

Hebrews 13:10–16

THE PERFECTION OF THE SHEPHERD

For the final time in the Book of Hebrews the writer brings up the issue of "perfection" or maturity. The word he used this time stresses the completion of all the Shepherd has begun in the lives of those in His flock.

For what did the writer of Hebrews request prayer for himself in these areas? (Heb. 13:18, 19)

In terms of his character

In terms of his conduct

In turn, for what did the writer of Hebrews pray concern ing his readers? (Heb. 13:21)

WORD WEALTH

Make you complete translates an important biblical word that has as its basic meaning "to arrange everything in the proper order for the best effect." Greek medical literature applied this word to setting broken bones. In the Gospels it is used of fishermen repairing their nets (Matt. 4:21). It isn't necessary for something to be broken for it to be "completed." In Hebrews 10:5 this word is used of the provision of a human body for Jesus. In Hebrews 13:21, the notion of the verb seems to be the harmonious application of all of the truth about the New Covenant—all that Christ died to provide and that He sits at the right hand of God to make real for His followers.

Why did the Hebrew Christians need the intervention of "the God of peace" on their behalf? (Heb. 13:20)

Why were all of the things the writer of Hebrews said about Jesus in his prayer important to the Hebrew Christians in their time of turmoil? (Heb. 13:20)

How did the writer of Hebrews evaluate the character of his epistle to the Hebrew Christians? (Heb. 13:22)

What do the final bits of personal information and greetings illustrate for the Hebrew Christians about the way the Shepherd completes the work He starts in the lives of His people? (Heb. 13:23–25)

 FAITH ALIVE

It is important to pray for spiritual leaders. What kinds of things should you pray about for them?

What area of your spiritual life would you like the great Shepherd of the sheep to bring into balanced and completed shape? Why?

What spiritual leader or mature Christian friend could you ask to pray for you and check up on you in the area of life mentioned in the previous question?

1. *Spirit-Filled Life Bible* (Nashville: Thomas Nelson Publishers, 1991), 1889, note on Hebrews 13:4.

2. Ibid., 1889, "Word Wealth: Hebrews 13:6, helper."

3. "Altar," *Nelson's Illustrated Bible Dictionary* (Nashville: Thomas Nelson Publishers, 1986), 37.

4. *Spirit-Filled Life Bible,* 1890, "Kingdom Dynamics: Hebrews 13:10–15, The Sacrifice of Praise."